Mexico's Energy Resources

Westview Replica Editions

The concept of Westview Replica Editions is a response to the continuing crisis in academic and informational publishing. Library budgets for books have been severely curtailed. Ever larger portions of general library budgets are being diverted from the purchase of books and used for data banks, computers, micromedia, and other methods of information retrieval. Interlibrary loan structures further reduce the edition sizes required to satisfy the needs of the scholarly community. Economic pressures on the university presses and the few private scholarly publishing companies have severely limited the capacity of the industry to properly serve the academic and research communities. As a result, many manuscripts dealing with important subjects, often representing the highest level of scholarship, are no longer economically viable publishing projects--or, if accepted for publication, are typically subject to lead times ranging from one to three years.

Westview Replica Editions are our practical solution to the problem. We accept a manuscript in camera-ready form, typed according to our specifications, and move it immediately into the production process. As always, the selection criteria include the importance of the subject, the work's contribution to scholarship, and its insight, originality of thought, and excellence of exposition. The responsibility for editing and proofreading lies with the author or sponsoring institution. We prepare chapter headings and display pages, file for copyright, and obtain Library of Congress Cataloging in Publication Data. A detailed manual contains simple instructions for preparing the final typescript, and our editorial staff is always available to answer questions.

The end result is a book printed on acid-free paper and bound in sturdy library-quality soft covers. We manufacture these books ourselves using equipment that does not require a lengthy make-ready process and that allows us to publish first editions of 300 to 600 copies and to reprint even smaller quantities as needed. Thus, we can produce Replica Editions quickly and can keep even very specialized books in print as long as there is a demand for them.

About the Book and Editors

Beginning from the premise that Mexico's economic strength will depend largely on its ability to produce, manage, and export energy, energy experts in this book analyze energy planning in Mexico in the 1970s and possible strategies for the future. They focus on the potential for diversifying the country's energy economy--now based almost exclusively on oil--by examining alternative sources, particularly natural gas, coal, and geothermal and solar resources. The extent to which Mexico's energy base is diversified, they assert, will determine the country's ability both to meet internal energy needs and to prolong its export of oil and gas. And, diversification will not only increase Mexico's economic strength, but will also expand the global supply of energy resources and have profound impact on the United States, Mexico's major trading partner.

Dr. Miguel S. Wionczek is a senior fellow and the head of the long-term energy research program at El Colegio de México. He is coeditor, with Gerald Foley and Ariane van Buren, of *Energy in the Transition from Rural Subsistence* (Westview, 1982). Dr. Ragaei El Mallakh is professor of economics and director of the International Research Center for Energy and Economic Development at the University of Colorado. He is the editor of the *Journal of Energy and Development* and *OPEC: Twenty Years and Beyond* (Westview, 1981).

Mexico's Energy Resources

Toward a Policy of Diversification

edited by Miguel S. Wionczek
and Ragaei El Mallakh

Routledge
Taylor & Francis Group
LONDON AND NEW YORK

First published 1985 by Westview Press, Inc.

Published 2018 by Routledge
52 Vanderbilt Avenue, New York, NY 10017
2 Park Square, Milton Park, Abingdon, Oxon OX14 4RN

Routledge is an imprint of the Taylor & Francis Group, an informa business

Library of Congress Cataloging in Publication Data
Mexico's energy resources.
(A Westview replica edition)
1. Power resources--Mexico. 2. Energy policy--Mexico.
I. Wionczek, Miguel S. II. El Mallakh, Ragaei,
1925- .
TJ163.25.M6M47 1985 333.79'0972 84-7399

ISBN 13: 978-0-367-01998-3 (hbk)
ISBN 13: 978-0-367-16985-5 (pbk)

Contents

Tables and Figures

TABLES

FIGURES

Mexico's Energy Resources

1
Current and Future Energy Options for Mexico

Ragaei El Mallakh

The idea for this volume first sprang from the August 1981 international conference on "Mexico: Energy Policy and Industrial Development," sponsored by the International Research Center for Energy and Economic Development (ICEED) and held at the University of Colorado, Boulder. At the conference the energy problems and industrialization issues of the country were presented by a number of participants. Afterward, several of the papers delivered at that conference were updated and expanded and now form the core of the book. Most papers, however, were prepared specifically for inclusion in this joint publication effort of El Colegio de Mexico and the ICEED.

In the few years that have passed since the conference, the pendulum has swung from boundless optimism concerning the future of Mexico based upon the accessibility of high levels of oil-generated revenues to fears of Mexican renunciation of or default on international debts. Since then, Mexico has inaugurated a new president, Miguel de la Madrid Hurtado, who took office in December 1982 and introduced an austerity program. Like the rest of the world, Mexico has suffered from spiraling inflation and the consequences of global recession.

When development and exploitation of Mexico's oil resources expanded rapidly in the 1970s, Mexico was frequently called the new Saudi Arabia. In actuality, only in the area of petroleum reserves could the two countries be compared. The most obvious difference is in the levels of domestic petroleum requirements and revenue needed to meet the demands of economic development. For starters, the population of Mexico City alone is more than ten times that of Saudi Arabia. This demographic indicator, coupled with a high birth rate and a rising standard of living, means that Mexican energy policy has to be geared primarily toward meeting ever-expanding domestic consumption. While meeting internal energy demand as efficiently as possible, Mexico must avoid the pitfall of overreliance on finite oil and gas reserves both for energy consumption and as a generator of revenues. If one were to compare

Mexico with a Middle Eastern oil-producing country, Egypt might offer a better analogy, although Mexican petroleum reserves and other energy resources are greater than those of Egypt.

"Petrolization" is a term used first by Mexican economists to describe the impact of rapid growth in petroleum output on their nation's economy. For many oil-producing countries, including those with developed economies such as Norway, there can be substantial negative effects of excessive reliance on the petroleum sector for economic growth and development.[1] The foreign trade of the countries dependent on petroleum exports has come of necessity to reflect the fluctuations--sometimes sharp--of the volatile world petroleum market. The miscalculation has been in assuming that all changes would be toward higher oil prices.

Somehow, there has been a tendency to exempt the oil industry from the consequences of business cycles. When a recession as deep and long-lasting as that of 1982-1984 occurs--the worst in four decades--the lower economic activity is mirrored in sharply reduced energy demand. Being no exception, Mexico's governmental revenues plummeted.

Another facet that tends to be underestimated is the close relationship between rapidly expanded oil revenues (on a large scale) and inflation. The experience of Mexico in the early 1980s indicates the seriousness of this problem and the necessity to follow moderation in petroleum output. From a producer's point of view, a moderate production policy ensures a longer life for the reserves, thereby extending over time the resource's benefits, and can serve to stabilize or even raise oil prices. In addition, there have been problems with crowding out nonpetroleum sectors in the economy, such as agriculture--a problem not unique to Mexico among the oil-producing countries. Even in the industrial sector the petroleum-based industries can garner the lion's share of investment capital, thereby distorting balanced growth within that sector. And aside from the danger of serious economic dependence on a single product, there are heavy social costs in excessive urbanization, expansion in bureaucracy, and the possibility of exacerbating maldistribution of wealth. Moreover, rapid expansion of oil output can lead to the accumulation of foreign debt to finance that expansion, which is exactly the problem confronting Mexico today.

ENERGY DEVELOPMENT AND THE DEBT BURDEN

By 1984, Mexican petroleum output was 300 percent above the production level of a decade earlier. This phenomenal increment was costly and is reflected in the fact that the direct debt incurred by Petroleos Mexicanos

(PEMEX), the state-owned oil company, represents about one-quarter of the nation's total indebtedness.[2] However, because of its sizable petroleum reserves (estimated for 1984 at 72.5 billion barrels),[3] Mexico has been more fortunate than other developing debtor countries during the recent recession. It has "underground collateral." Morever, by the end of 1984 a modest international economic recovery is expected to raise oil demand and, even under the assumption of no major changes in the nominal price of oil through 1985, the value of oil exports of the major producing countries, including Mexico, is expected to rise.[4]

Although the development of energy--and particularly of petroleum--has absorbed a major portion of expenditures in the industrial sector, energy stands as the major foreign exchange earner. Oil and gas exports account for 75 percent of Mexico's total merchandise exports. Since 1983 there has been an improvement in Mexico's balance of payments; in that year the Central Bank increased its foreign exchange reserves by more than $3 billion and had a trade surplus of about $14 billion. Improvement in the trade sector has continued into 1984.

In his State of the Union address in early September 1984, President de la Madrid outlined the government's priorities and thrusts to put the economy back on an even keel. The two major objectives are to continue to combat inflationary pressures and to reduce sharply governmental expenditures. Inflation has been targeted as the premier villain, not only because of its consequences for Mexicans, but because the added interest costs have consumed a large portion of the country's financial resources, thereby diverting investment from development programs. Already strides have been made to curb inflation, with the annual rate for 1984 expected to be about half the rates of the preceding years.[5]

In August 1984 Mexico and its foreign bank creditors completed a tentative agreement, considered a major breakthrough, on debt repayment. This agreement stipulates that Mexico will undertake repayment of its debts over a period of fourteen years at a lowered interest rate.[6] Stretching out repayment of debts (including principal payments due through 1990) will substantially ease the Mexican financial crisis and allow for better management with lessened tensions and stress.

THE EVOLVING MEXICAN POLICY

Mexico's energy policy guidelines appear to concentrate on (1) diversification, (2) expanded processing capabilities in petroleum, (3) greater efficiency in domestic consumption, and (4) stability in pricing. In diversification (to be discussed in greater detail in the following chapters), a resource selected for major development attention has been natural gas. A part of the rationale for expanding natural gas demand and supply is to reduce the waste in gas produced in association with crude oil, representing 80 percent of Mexico's natural gas, and to meet the growth in domestic energy demand. From 1976 to 1983, domestic consumption of natural gas grew at an annual rate of 10 percent; in the three-year span 1977-1980, that rate was almost 19 percent, traceable to fuel switching and to overall rising demand for energy. Given the priority assigned to natural gas as a domestic energy source, exports have been kept to about 10 percent of total supply. A 1985 PEMEX target is to reduce flaring of gas to 2 percent of gross output. Over a five-year period natural gas production is projected to increase only moderately, by 150 billion cubic feet per day as of 1988. That increment should easily meet the expected 5 percent annual growth rate in domestic demand for natural gas during that half decade. PEMEX has made major strides in reducing gas flared in association with the lifting of crude oil. In 1976 nearly 500 million cubic feet per day--almost a quarter of total gas produced--was flared. By 1981 that figure had been reduced to 16 percent.[7]

In refining capacity, Mexico has moved forward swiftly and has effected a turnaround from the conditions prevailing before 1980 when the country imported more refined products than it exported. Only two years earlier (1978), Mexican product imports were running at 14.5 million barrels, its total oil production was 307.9 million barrels, and its product exports were only 0.7 million barrels.[8] The recession in the early 1980s brought reduced demand for oil products, particularly gasoline, which resulted in the deferring of some planned refinery expansion.

Increased efficiency of energy consumption is being sought not only on economic grounds to prolong the life of Mexico's hydrocarbon reserves but also because of environmental concerns. In May 1983 PEMEX began an active policy for environmental protection together with the Ministry of Urban Development and Ecology (SUDUE). The national oil company expects to budget around 177 million pesos for repair of the environmental damage caused by its operations, such as that from hydrocarbon spills. Perhaps more difficult to implement are pollution control measures in the transport sector in general and for the Valley of Mexico (with Mexico City) in particular. By the mid-1980s a monitoring system in the Valley of Mexico should be operational, along with a drive to substitute natural gas for fuel oil in electrical power-generating plants in the area and to upgrade automotive and diesel fuels.

In the area of pricing, Mexico's energy policy looks toward stability. To this end, there has been an effective level of informal coordination between Mexico and the Organization of the Petroleum Exporting Countries

(OPEC) during the critical 1983 period of the OPEC London meeting and on subsequent occasions throughout that year and into 1984. The level of oil prices is a key issue not only in maintaining an element of stability in revenues to allow for the orderly implementation of development programs but also with an eye to lessening the possibility of economically premature substitution of certain energy sources for oil and gas.

The worldwide recession, falling oil prices, and plummeting oil-generated revenues all contributed to the elaboration of Mexico's 1984-1988 National Energy Plan (NEP). Announced in August 1984, the NEP supports continuing the 1.5 million barrel per day oil export ceiling but subject to possible revision. It also calls for keeping intact the guideline to diversify the purchasers of Mexican petroleum by selling no more than half of Mexico's exports to any one country and holding those exports to 20 percent of the purchasing nation's total oil imports.

The NEP projects an annual growth in crude oil output of 3.5 percent during the plan period (1985-1988) above the 2.7 million barrels per day in 1984, with natural gas production rising at 2.5 percent per year over the 1984 level of 4.043 billion cubic feet per day. Refining capacity is targeted to rise from 1.868 million barrels per day in 1984 to 2.3 million barrels per day in 1988.[9]

The NEP has reemphasized the diversification of Mexico's energy sources with the goal of reducing the country's reliance on oil and natural gas from the 1984 level of 93 percent to 73 percent by the year 2000. If the energy plan is aggressively implemented, primary energy production from solid fuels and geothermal resources should grow by 16.5 percent and 17.5 percent, respectively, from 1984 to 1988. Even with such expansion, these sources would meet only 3 percent and 0.7 percent, respectively, of the nation's total energy requirements. Hydroelectric power output would be raised to maintain its 5 percent share in the energy supply. Only 30 percent of Mexico's potential hydroelectric generating capacity is being used as of 1984. However, hydroelectric projects tend to be expensive, large, and require long construction times for the generating facilities and distribution grids. Finally, although nuclear power had been downgraded earlier, the NEP supports implementation of the first and second stages of the Laguna Verde nuclear project with a completion date in 1988. The plan involves the eventual construction of four to five additional nuclear facilities on the Laguna Verde scale (1,350 MW).[10]

In conclucion, although the current energy options for Mexico are constrained by the global recession, a temporarily slackened petroleum demand, lower revenues, and a sizable debt burden, Mexico's future options in energy are more promising. The country has substantial potential in hydroelectric power, geothermal energy, and, to a lesser extent, in coal. Mexico's significant reserves of oil and natural gas can continue to provide an engine for development of the economy and, because of the nonrenewable nature of hydrocarbons, for development of alternative energy supplies.

NOTES

1. The Mexican and Norwegian oil development experiences have been reviewed in Ragaei El Mallakh, Barry W. Poulson, and Øystein Noreng, *Petroleum and Economic Development: The Cases of Mexico and Norway* (Lexington, Mass.: D. C. Heath and Company, 1983).

2. Interview with Mario Ramon Beteta, director-general of PEMEX in *Business Week*, August 13, 1984, p. 56.

3. Of the 72.5 billion barrels, 69 percent is in oil. Petroleos Mexicanos, New York and Washington Representative Office, *PEMEX Information Bulletin*, July 1984, p. 7.

4. International Monetary Fund (IMF), *World Economic Outlook* (Washington, D.C.: IMF, 1984), p. 48.

5. *Wall Street Journal*, section 2, September 4, 1984.

6. The specifics would include fourteen years for Mexico to repay the $20 billion in principal that will fall due through 1989 and that has not yet been rescheduled, along with a one-year grace period. In addition, Mexico's $11.5 billion in already rescheduled principal that will fall due in 1987 and 1988 would be repaid over twelve years (without a grace period). Those rescheduled payments on $11.5 billion falling due in 1989 and 1990 will be repayable over ten years (without a grace period). A London-based interest rate would be charged rather than being based upon the more erratically fluctuating U.S. prime rate. *New York Times*, business section, August 28, 1984.

7. George Baker, *Mexico's Petroleum Sector* (Tulsa, Okla.: PennWell Books, 1984), p. 52.

8. Jesus-Agustin Velasco-S., *Impacts of Mexican Oil Policy on Economic and Political Development* (Lexington, Mass.: D. C. Heath and Company, 1983), p. 70.

9. Government of Mexico, *Plan Nacional de Energeticos, 1984-1988*, 1984.

10. Ibid.

2
Mexican Economic and Oil Policies of the 1970s and Strategies for the 1980s

Roberto Gutierrez

The development strategy that promoted the Mexican economy to its present semi-industrialized state did not arise spontaneously. As in most Latin American countries, it was provoked by and represented a reversal of the initial development model, which promoted primary products exports and is sometimes referred to as outward-directed growth. The change in policy was effected in response to the crisis suffered by the world capitalist system in the period from 1929 to 1932, which led to a shrinking of international markets and forced countries that exported raw materials to undertake industrial production.[1]

Industrialization in Mexico was facilitated by President Lazaro Cardenas (1934-1940). Confronted with the need to incorporate several marginal sectors into the national economy, his administration contributed to the expansion of the domestic market and laid the foundations of the industrialization process--effectively setting the course for the Mexican economy from the 1940s onward. In sum, the origins of the current model of development date back to the 1930s, although consolidation of the import-substitution process, the break with the export-led model, and the initiation of industrialization did not occur until after World War II.[2]

The import-substitution process, which has been in effect from 1945 until the present, has had two stages: the first (from 1945 to the mid-1960s) was the "easy" import-substitution period; and the second (since the mid-1960s) is the "difficult" stage of import substitution, which corresponds to the maturing of what is known as the stabilizing development model. This second stage is of particular importance here, as it constitutes the point of departure for this chapter. During this stage, the momentum of import substitution was arrested, leading many observers to voice serious doubts about the strategy and to suggest that it be replaced. Criticisms were first raised in 1974; even sharper criticism followed in 1976 and 1977, when the Mexican economy suffered its first really significant recession since the beginning of the industrialization process. Indictments of the inward-directed growth strategy no longer resided only in its having been restricted to the import substitution of non-durable consumer goods and its not having been firmly established with regard to intermediate and capital goods; criticism extended to include the fact that certain key branches of industrial activity had shown clear regressive tendencies, registering a fall in import-substitution rates.[3] As a result, the current account deficit in the balance of payments and the foreign debt rose to very high levels.

It was by a process of elimination and, in part, imitation that Mexico and other Latin American countries opted for the import-substitution model with the aim of achieving self-sustained domestic development. This choice was implicit in the process of eliminating some industrial imports and the only apparent option to follow after the failure of the outward-directed growth model during the great depression. Moreover, it was adopted in imitation of the growth path of the more advanced countries. Inherent in the adoption of this new model was what might now be considered the pure Rostowian theory, which postulated that by copying the industrialization stages of the developed countries, developing countries could achieve comparable levels of economic and social well-being. This approach did make possible, to a certain extent, comparable accumulation patterns, but consumption patterns similar to those experienced by the developed countries have never been achieved in view of the limited nature of Latin American domestic markets. It had been hoped that the import-substitution process would be fully completed by the end of the 1960s, at which time Latin America was to have achieved greater financial independence, stand considerably closer to self-sufficiency in production in all sectors, and have built up sufficient capacity to produce manufactured and even other types of goods with greater value added that would be competitive on international markets.[4] Today it is generally agreed not only that the model's linear dimensions are an oversimplification but also that the model's unfavorable effects were underestimated, particularly with regard to its effects on income concentration, structural heterogeneity, and imbalance between sectors and between regions and in the balance of payments.

Looking back, it is apparent that dependence on the industrialized nations had merely changed in character. During the period of outward-directed growth, the industrialized markets had been needed as outlets for production; during the period of inward-directed growth there was a particular need for the direct investment, science, technology, and financial capital of the industrialized nations.

In keeping with the import-substitution process, Mexico and other Latin American countries threw open their borders to transnational capital and allowed the virtual unconditional entry of foreign firms who would produce within their borders those goods that had been previously imported. After a few years, countries in the area became aware that they had not only mortgaged a major part of their economies to these companies, but also that their economic and financial imbalances in relation to other countries were largely caused by these companies. The surplus from direct foreign investment soon became a deficit.[5] The international capital that was introduced into the region under conditions of high security became astonishingly volatile when, for political reasons, this security appeared to weaken. This phenomenon persists to this day.

The appropriateness of the particular forms of direct investment was questionable. Insufficient care was taken in the selection of imported technology in terms of its suitability to the needs of the region, particularly with regard to the use of labor. Until recently, little attention has been given to the problem of unemployment. The agricultural sector in Mexico was strong until the 1960s, when the migration of labor from rural to urban areas served to stimulate the industrialization process. In many instances, the "key in hand" formula was accepted, whereby imported technology is transferred without any adaptation being made. In some cases, even the simplest components required for the installation of manufacturing plants were imported. In other cases, products were manufactured domestically but using foreign technology.

It was not until the 1970s that Mexican legislation regarding the appropriateness and responsibility of foreign investment was thoroughly revised. But Mexico was not unique in this respect. No Latin American country had a scientific and technological institutional framework equal to forecasting the future need for trained technical personnel or capable of developing production processes in keeping with the needs of their economies. The Japanese "miracle" achieved primarily by copying or adapting foreign technology had only recently been accomplished and could not, therefore, be taken as a model.

The imbalances in production and the need to import goods and services in order to lend continuity to the development model produced permanent deficits on current account in the balance of payments. These deficits could only be financed by incurring foreign debt, making dependence still more pronounced. With the passage of time, the amounts involved in debt servicing rose to levels almost equal to the income generated from new financing. It became common practice to contract loans to service the debt, a process known as "the vicious circle of indebtedness."

THE TRADITIONAL POLE OF DEVELOPMENT

From the 1960s onward, when funds flowed into manufacturing plants, the sector that became the most dynamic pole and principal indicator of income concentration in Mexico was that of durable consumer goods production (automobiles, household goods, electrical domestic appliances). This may be explained as much by the speed of its response to changes in the economy's spending capacity as by the fact that it was geared toward the middle-to-high income bracket. The main characteristics of the sector that produces durable consumer goods are:

1. Production levels based on demand in those sectors of society where the greatest share of income is concentrated.
2. Broad and intensive marketing compaigns that raise the cost of this type of goods and facilitate an increase in sales price, producing a particularly large profit margin for a very limited number of companies that are generally based on transnational capital.
3. Credit facilities to buyers to promote sales.
4. Continuous modification of the goods produced in order to base competition on differentiation in products rather than on price.
5. A small number of consumers per type of product, which, on the one hand, permits a high cost for each type of goods produced (or each product model) and, on the other, permits a very large number of models in relation to the size of the market.
6. Barriers to the entry of new companies into the market, with entry determined principally by the available amount of starting capital, the degree of technological innovation, access to raw materials and suitable factors of production, and the availability of both domestic and foreign financing.

A look at the dynamics of the sector producing durable consumer goods during the 1970s, as compared to those of other sectors, allows us to appreciate to what extent the sector has become the backbone of the Mexican model of economic development (see Table 2.1). With the exception of the years 1976 and 1977, the rate of growth in the production of durable consumer goods exceeded that of the gross domestic product (GDP), nondurable consumer goods, manufactured goods as a whole, and the entire industrial sector. The average rate of growth in the production of durable consumer goods from 1972 to 1980 stood at 10.2 percent, whereas GDP grew at 5.8 percent, the industrial sector at 7.1 percent, and manufactured goods at 6.4 percent.

A prime example of the dynamics of the durable consumer goods producing industry is that of automobile

Table 2.1
Annual Percentage Variation in Industrial Production and GDP, 1972-1980

	1972	1973	1974	1975	1976	1977	1978	1979	1980	AGR*
GDP	7.3	7.6	5.9	4.2	1.7	3.2	7.0	8.0	7.4	5.8
Industry	9.3	8.9	7.2	4.7	2.7	3.5	10.0	10.3	7.8	7.1
Manufactured goods	8.3	8.7	6.7	4.0	2.8	3.4	8.8	9.2	5.6	6.4
Consumer goods	8.1	8.3	4.3	4.3	2.4	4.2	7.0	9.3	4.8	5.8
Nondurable	7.8	7.2	2.5	3.9	2.8	5.5	5.0	7.4	3.1	5.0
Durable	10.7	15.3	14.5	6.6	0.6	3.4	18.4	18.8	12.7	10.2

*AGR = average growth rate

Source: Banco de Mexico, *Annual Report*, various issues.

production, the strongest branch of the industry. After registering negative growth rates of an average 8.9 percent between 1975 and 1977, it reported positive rates of 29.3 percent, 16.8 percent, and 6.4 percent in 1978, 1979, and 1980, respectively (whereas GDP rose by 7.0 percent, 8.0 percent, and 7.4 percent, respectively). This demonstrates the high GDP elasticity for both increases and decreases of this branch of the industry and also serves to identify it as the beneficiary of the reactivation of the Mexican economy over the last few years.

However, the dynamics of the durable consumer goods producing sector do not correspond to the pace of income accumulation and distribution of welfare in society. Profits deriving from the production of these goods have been concentrated in a very small sector of the population, in such a way that only a fraction of the surplus obtained has circulated to the most disadvantaged strata of society. Because many studies have analyzed the ensuing problems of employment, income distribution, concentration of economic activity, structural heterogeneity, and imbalance between sectors, they will not be treated in this chapter.[6]

THE NEW POLE OF DEVELOPMENT

It is clear that the traditional pole of the development model is highly vulnerable to any drop in demand. This model requires continuous outside stimuli, which bleeds the economy. The Mexican government became fully aware of this in the late 1970s, as is apparent from its fiscal modifications made in 1979 and 1980 and the temporary ruling out of any possibility of Mexico's joining the General Agreement on Tariffs and Trade (GATT). An attempt has been initiated to make the productive apparatus and the income-generating mechanisms in Mexico self-sufficient. Means have been sought to increase domestic savings and to reformulate the traditional import-substitution model. Economic policy has been constantly modified, but the principal change to have been instituted by the state in the late 1970s has been to make endogenous the variable central core of the accumulation model. This is of crucial importance and lays down a clear framework for economic development in Mexico in the future, the forthcoming economic and financial crisis notwithstanding.

In thereby assuming control of the development model, the state has partially deprived the private sector of this priviledge. The durable consumer goods industry is no longer the most dynamic or, at least, no longer the industry that most closely reflects overall growth trends. Over the past few years, it has had to share this role with the hydrocarbon-exporting element of the oil industry. It is important to remember how this change originated and developed.

The economy's inherent contradictions that had accumulated during the period of inward-directed growth gave rise in 1976 to the need to effect major changes in Mexico's financial and trade relations with other countries. Negotiations with the International Monetary Fund (IMF) caused the foreign debt of the public sector to lose importance for some time as a balancing factor in the current account deficit in the balance of payments. It was necessary to strengthen the economy's foreign exchange generating capacity. Here a review should be made of the principal current account deficit figures and those showing the indebtedness causing the disequilibrium in Mexico's balance of trade over the recent past.[7]

1. The current account deficit in the balance of payments accumulated between 1951 and 1980 (1955 was the only year in which a surplus was registered) and in 1980 stood at more than $50 trillion, of which more than 80 percent was incurred during the 1970s.
2. The deficit share in GDP rose from an annual average of 1.7 percent during the 1960s to 3.0 percent during the 1970s.
3. The accumulated foreign debt of the public sector increased from 12.7 percent of GDP in 1970 to 25.5 percent in 1979 (in 1977 this figure reached the unprecedented level of 30.9 percent).
4. The coefficient of solvency (total servicing of the debt divided by goods and services exported) rose from 0.26 in 1970 to 0.62 in 1979. If this trend continues for a further six years, conceivably the total income from exports will have to be employed in servicing the foreign debt.
5. From 1976 onward, the balance on services account ceased to show a surplus, due, to a large extent, to high interest payments on the foreign debt; for this reason the deficit on current account as a whole began to increase (both the services and trade balance).

In view of these contradictions, Mexico turned to a new pole of development accomodating more efficient currency generation. The arguments advanced by the government for placing hydrocarbons exports in this role center on certain considerations, although the views presented herein do not necessarily coincide with those held by the author. Below are some of the reasons posited for assigning an important role to hydrocarbons export.

1. There was a large increase in proven hydrocarbon reserves disclosed from the early months of the Lopez Portillo administration onward.
2. Petroleos Mexicanos (PEMEX) employs the largest

work force in Mexico and expansion of the company would generate further jobs, both in the oil industry itself and in other branches of the economy.

3. The apparent absence of near-term close hydrocarbon substitutes might lead to a drop in oil consumption on the international market (inelastic demand). For this reason--it was thought in Mexico--there was nothing to stop the national oil company from becoming an important world market supplier. The only obstacles with which PEMEX might have had to contend (technology and financing) were overcome through long experience as an independent enterprise and the company's easy access to loans since it possessed long-term resources with which to make repayments.
4. There was security inherent in the knowledge that hydrocarbon resources were controlled by Mexican personnel and know-how (PEMEX was the first oil industry of the Third World to be nationalized). Therefore, it seemed feasible to rationally plan the exploitation and disposition of oil, in keeping with the overall objectives of national development, and it was possible to prevent the situation arising, as it did in the case of durable consumer goods, wherein expansion of the industry was undertaken in accordance with the interests of foreign firms or investors.[8]
5. It was possible to keep the price elasticity of demand for hydrocarbons low over a prolonged period, thereby ensuring a relatively broader profit margin in international sales than for other products exported by Mexico.
6. The short-term viability of oil contributed to the solution of the long-standing problems to which the Mexican economy had been subject and reduced the social pressures to which these gave rise.[9]

It was furthermore agreed that higher income and employment levels of the labor force should be made basic objectives of economic development in Mexico. Theoretically, these two objectives are complementary: a national increase in income implies an increase in levels of employment. The strategy implemented to acheive this end was an attempt to influence national expenditure decisions in certain areas, such as personal consumption, private investment, government expenditure, and foreign trade.

Oil initially offered the possibility of attacking existing economic problems on the dual fronts of foreign indebtedness and public expenditure. The major state expenditures required to strengthen the productive capacity of PEMEX had the advantage of producing ample returns, giving results in a relatively short time through hydrocarbons exports. Subsequently, the multiplier effect of government expenditure and the security of having available plentiful supplies of resources of high international value, together with certain major measures of economic policy, among them the freezing of domestic energy prices, allowed the two remaining components, namely personal consumption and private investment, to be given new momentum. The overall increase in the components of total gross expenditure produced the economic structure to be seen in Mexico today.

AN OIL-DOMINATED ECONOMY

The most painful, although not necessarily the most worrying, cost of oil expansion in Mexico has been inflation. Whereas the growth rate stood at 7 percent in 1978, 8 percent in 1979, and 7.4 percent in 1980, inflation rates increased by 17 percent, 22 percent, and 30 percent, respectively. Hence, on average, inflation rose by three points for every point increase in GDP, a 3:1 ratio. During the 1960s, this ratio had been less than unity and even during the first six years of the 1970s, when Mexico was apparently approaching its first grave recession since the great depression, it was 2:1. According to preliminary figures, the economy's total demand in the late 1970s increased 1.5 times more rapidly than the supply of total goods and services. It is obvious that income from oil is not solely responsible for inflation. Inflation is caused in part by the prices of imported goods and factors of production, higher value-added tax introduced in 1980, inelasticity of supply in various branches and sectors of the economy (bottlenecks), an exorbitant increase in the rates of interest, the freedom enjoyed by the commercial sector in fixing prices of goods and services, and even consumer psychology.

The problem of bottlenecks has been particularly serious. Since 1978, the World Bank recognized this constraint and suggested that Mexico open its economy and thereby eliminate most bottlenecks. The World Bank has also intimated that all goods and services may be imported, with the exception of certain goods and services that it would not be feasible to acquire abroad, such as those related specifically to the energy, transport, and construction sectors. The bank also insisted that if demand were not met, inflation would increase. Moreover, what could Mexico do with the foreign currency it was earning other than import resources from abroad?[10]

Mexico has, to a certain extent, acted on these suggestions. Although the government chose not to enter GATT, in 1980 Mexico lowered import tariffs and eliminated many of the import permits that were previously required "in any branch of activity in which domestic supply was recognized to be inadequate."[11] By the end of the same year, imported nondurable and luxury manufactures, besides capital and intermediate goods, saturated Mexico's market.

The sector suffering most seriously from the insufficient domestic supply was that of agriculture. This sector of the economy recorded its highest-ever level of imports over the past few years and in 1980, for the first time, registered a negative balance in its trade with other countries. According to preliminary figures, agricultural imports during that year exceeded 8.5 million tons, accounting for 16 percent of the total value of imports.[12]

Growth of the industrial sector dropped to 7.8 percent in 1980, following its reactivation in 1978 and 1979 and the growth rates of 10 percent and 9.5 percent, respectively. The most noticeable impact was on manufactured goods (growth in this branch standing at 5.6 percent), which was reflected in a decline in the share of these goods in total exports. This was further apparent in the fact that the growth of nonoil exports, at current prices, in 1980 stood at only 1.3 percent above the 1979 level, constituting a drop in real terms. Although the Mexican economy worked at full capacity, events have shown that the infrastructure of ports was inadequate and the railway network was deficient and obsolete (more than 3,000 loaded railcars remained halted at the northern border until the beginning of 1981). The unrealized transportation linkages affected the iron and steel, cement, oil, and petrochemical equipment and other capital goods industries, making it necessary to make major purchases abroad in order to avoid breaking the rate of growth of the economy or sacrificing the anticipated oil production rate of 2.7 million b/d (barrels of crude oil per day) for 1981. The fact that since 1970 80 percent of all import purchases consisted of production-related goods (in 1980 this figure reached 87 percent as is shown in Table 2.2) indicated that bottlenecks continued to exist in the industrial sector and that the import-substitution process in the case of intermediate and capital goods suffered from the stagnation and technological backwardness of the 1970s. This situation may be justified in the short term in the interests of high growth rates but constitutes a serious obstacle to the future of the Mexican economy.

By 1980 the Mexican administration assumed that the international oil boom would last forever and that proceeds from growing oil exports would assure the country continuous and self-sustained economic growth.[13] In many circles the idea was entertained that besides stepping up the import of resources and even increasing direct and indirect investment abroad, Mexico would be obliged to use the foreign currency produced from oil in new ways. The most viable short-term possibilities considered at that time were the anticipatory payment of a large part of the public sector's foreign debt and intensification of programs of joint investment with other countries to strengthen domestic physical infrastructure and industrial

Table 2.2
Structure of Mexican Imports, 1970-1980 (millions of dollars)

	1970	1972	1974	1976	1977	1978	1979	1980
Consumer goods	528	608	676	311	417	447	1,002	2,426
Production-related goods	1,932	2,110	4,733	5,216	4,624	7,267	10,983	16,146
Raw and auxiliary materials	798	918	3,007	2,706	2,537	5,286	7,406	11,028
Investment goods	1,134	1,192	1,726	2,510	2,087	1,981	3,577	5,118
Unclassified	--	--	647	503	849	--	--	--
Total	2,460	2,718	6,057	6,030	5,890	7,714	11,985	18,572

Note: Totals have been rounded off and therefore may not add up.

Source: Banco de Mexico, *Annual Report*, various issues.

plants.[14] Furthermore, it was maintained that the relatively stable share of the public sector's foreign debt in GDP over the previous few years was an indication that Mexico had achieved a high degree of financial self-sufficiency.[15] The domestic savings/GDP coefficient increased from 19 percent in 1976 to 23 percent in 1980.[16] It was postulated that when this coefficient reached the considered optimum level of 27 percent, Mexico would be able to dispense with the need to incur foreign debt and would be able, if it so desired, to settle part of existing foreign debt commitments in advance.[17]

In this atmosphere of unlimited optimism, many possibilities were debated domestically and abroad about stepping up programs of joint investment between Mexico and other countries. The urgent needs that became apparent in the short term with respect to joint investment projects were the electrification of the railway network; construction of the second stage of the Lazaro Cardenas-Las Truchas iron and steel plant; rail links between the ports of Coatzacoalcos and Salina Cruz across the Tehuantepec Isthmus (Alpha-Omega project); construction of four industrial ports as specified in the National Industrial Development Plan (Tampico, Coatzacoalcos, Lazaro Cardenas-Las Truchas, and Salina Cruz); expansion of crude oil storage capacity in the Mexican Gulf; expansion of the oil port of Pajaritos in the state of Veracruz; construction of plants to produce wide-diameter pipes; construction of the oil port of Dos Bocas in the state of Tabasco; installation of new collective transport system networks (metro) in the Federal District; and strengthening of the food industry. Many of these projects were started in 1980-1981 and involved large external financial commitments and a rapidly increasing external debt to be paid with future oil revenues.

Some critical voices had insisted that if the dynamics of the industrial expansion and the 8 percent growth rate were to be maintained through the 1980s, as specified in the development programs elaborated in the second half of the 1970s, there was no alternative but to continue to increase the volume of hydrocarbon exports under the conditions of the international oil boom.[18] Such a policy would heighten the mono-export trend to which the country was already subject by 1979-1980, when the export of oil and its by-products accounted for two-thirds of the total volume of goods exported. Crude oil alone represented 61 percent of this total, as is shown in Table 2.3.

A conceptual discussion emerged about what constituted "mono-exporter." As a rule, a country is taken to be a mono-exporter when more than 50 percent of its foreign sales are of a single product or commodity. According to a definition advanced by the World Bank, an oil country is one in which at least three-quarters of exports consist of oil. Hence, by 1979-1980, Mexico was on the verge of becoming an oil mono-exporter, if it was not already.

Table 2.3
Structure of Mexican Exports, 1970-1980[a] (millions of dollars)

	1970	1972	1974	1975	1976[p]	1977[p]	1978[p]	1979[p]	1980[p]
Agriculture, livestock, forestry, and fisheries	621.2	786.3	802.5	814.8	1,185.8	1,439.0	1,600.2	1,943.8	1,544.0
Extration industries	216.2	201.9	465.0	737.8	834.8	1,288.4	2,093.9	4,008.9	10,381.0
Oil and its by-products	38.4	21.4	123.2	460.0	557.0	1,029.4	1,805.0	3,789.3	9,429.6
Metals and metalloids	177.9	280.5	341.8	277.7	277.9	259.0	288.9	219.6	951.8
Manufacturing industries	443.9	677.0	1,434.3	1,186.9	1,190.8	1,611.0	2,008.9	2,446.7	3,378.8
Unclassified	--	--	148.1	121.5	104.4	79.8	120.3	156.3	3.2
Total	1,281.3	1,665.2	2,850.0	2,861.0	3,315.8	4,418.4	5,832.2	8,555.5	15,307.0

[a]the activities of assembly companies excluded; reevaluation included.

p = preliminary

Note: Totals have been rounded off and therefore may not add up.

Source: Banco de Mexico, S. A., *Economic Indicators*, several issues: Coodinacion General del Sistema Nacional de Informacion de la Secretaria de Programacion y Presupuesto (General Office of the National Information System of the Department of Programming and Budgeting).

The economy would have been hard put for even a partial reversal of this trend: crude oil exports would have to be kept to 1 million b/d and the export of other products increased more than 10 percent per year by 1985 or soon thereafter to reduce oil exports to 50 percent. This would obviously be difficult since the Energy Program laid down more ambitious oil export figures. Furthermore, it would be economically unsound to leave idle the capacity established with the intent to increase crude production. The problem no longer lay in seeking to export 1.5 million b/d of crude oil, but rather in exceeding this figure.[19] What practically nobody took into consideration at the policy level was that in the light of international economic developments, there was no guarantee that the worldwide oil boom would last.

The events following the spring of 1981 proved that the 1970s oil boom would not last. By the winter of 1981-1982, Mexico found itself facing an economic and financial crisis much more serious than that of 1975-1976.

However, during what proved to be the final stages of the boom, there was much talk of the new negotiating power enjoyed by Mexico because of its oil. In late 1980, when exportable crude surpluses barely reached 1 million b/d,[20] commitments had already been made for 1.5 million b/d for export (see Table 2.4). Rather than assuming that increased oil sales imply increased bargaining power, policy makers in Mexico should have watched the developments of international hydrocarbon markets and the world economy. In view of the size of its population and its geographical location, Mexico--even without its oil--is an important country in the eyes of the industrial powers affected by protracted economic stagnation. Domestic growth targets and policies for negotiating with other countries should have been reexamined at the right moment since, if the same expansionary policy based upon oil exports was to be followed under less and less favorable international conditions, hydrocarbon sales commitments would have to be increased still further with few new buyers in sight. Moreover, even if one accepts that oil provides greater bargaining power, it does not necessarily imply increased economic independence under conditions of world economic instability. Quite the contrary: because the main problems arising from oil-related foreign earnings are in administrative capacity and technology, dependence on other countries under the general conditions of economic uncertainity is bound to increase rather than diminish.

Some observers of the national scene in 1980-1981 have pointed out that although the trend toward mono-exporting (and even mono-exporting itself) may not be too serious since it can be reversed, a problem resides in the domestic and external effects of mono-production. Analyses of the mono-production problem are generally based on the experiences of the Organization of the

Table 2.4
Program for Mexican Crude Oil Exports, 1981

	Barrels (per day)	Share (percent)
United States	733,000	48.8
Spain	220,000	14.6
Japan	100,000	6.7
France	100,000	6.7
Sweden	70,000	4.7
Canada	50,000	3.3
Israel	45,000	3.0
Brazil	40,000	2.7
India	30,000	2.0
Jamaica	13,000	0.9
Panama	12,000	0.8
Philippines	10,000	0.6
Guatemala	7,500	0.5
Costa Rica	7,500	0.5
Nicaragua	7,500	0.5
El Salvador	7,000	0.5
Honduras	6,000	0.4
Haiti	3,500	0.2
Yugoslavia	3,000	0.2
Others	35,000	2.3
Total (approx.)	1,500,000	100.0

Source: Secretaria de Programacion y Presupuesto, *Expenditure Budget of the Federation,* 1981.

Petroleum Exporting Countries (OPEC) members, where the industrialization process has been rather slow and disappointing. If appropriate measures are not taken, the situation in Mexico could deteriorate as easily as it did in 1981-1982. It is for this reason that certain experts inside and outside the administration were advocating in 1980-1981 a number of measures: the diversification of manufactured goods, the application of more highly labor-intensive techniques, a slowdown of the process of increased dependence on imports from abroad,[21] a strengthening of the agricultural sector, the stimulation of capital goods production, the formulation of a coherent and viable policy for science and technology,[22] the implementation of an effective selection process for direct foreign investment, and, in general, a rethinking of the import-substitution policy.

Of the entire range of problems with which the Mexican economy has been faced, the inability to employ sufficient labor continues to be the most serious: open employment stands at 8 percent and disguised unemployment at 47.5 percent of the economically active population. High rates of growth must be maintained if jobs are to be created, although it is calculated that full employment could be achieved by the end of this century if the current annual average level of labor absorption of 4.2 percent is maintained (a goal established in the 1980-1982 National Employment Program).[23]

One of the principal back-up measures was the strengthening of the agriculture sector, through which it was hoped to attain the triple objectives of boosting production, achieving food self-sufficiency, and, by providing jobs, discouraging rural-to-urban migration. The main instrument for achieving these ends was the Mexican Food System (SAM), which sought, with very limited success, to guarantee self-sufficiency in basic foodstuffs through state intervention in marketing and shared-risk credit processes, together with other measures, such as the rehabilitation of irrigation areas and the Law of Agricultural Development--aimed at increasing the productivity of the rural population and pushing back agricultural frontiers.[24] In both cases, the introduction of more advanced technology and the provision of improved seeds and fertilizers were considered of utmost importance. Therefore, a considerable proportion of income from oil was channeled toward this sector. The draft Expenditure Budget of the Federation for 1981 stipulated that the agricultural sector would, during the course of that year, absorb 25 percent of total oil earnings, that is, some 66.6 billion Mexican pesos (Table 2.5).

The economy's widening range of imbalances and needs made it difficult to renounce the objective of maintaining high rates of growth. Policy consisted of alternately boosting and restraining the economy, a technique known in the industrial countries as a "stop and go" policy.

Table 2.5
Total Amount and Uses of Oil Earnings, 1980-1981

	1980		1981	
	Pesos (millions)	Percent	Pesos (millions)	Percent
Income from oil	211.6	100.0	417.8	100.0
PEMEX savings	55.3	26.1	151.3	36.2
Export tax[a]	156.3	73.9	266.5	63.8
Allocation	211.6	100.0	417.8	100.0
PEMEX investment[b]	55.3	26.1	151.3	36.2
Expenditure other sectors	156.3	73.9	266.5	63.8
Agriculture	38.2	18.1	66.6	15.9
Communications and transport	31.2	14.7	53.3	12.8
Social welfare	37.5	17.7	64.0	15.3
Industry, except PEMEX	23.9	11.3	42.6	10.2
States and municipalities	25.5	12.1	40.0	9.6

[a]In addition, PEMEX paid domestic taxes totaling 29.7 and 41.0 billion Mexican pesos in 1980 and 1981, respectively.

[b]This constitutes 44.5% and 97.2% of the total PEMEX Investment Program for 1980 and 1981, respectively.

Source: Secretaria de Programacion y Presupuesto, *Expenditure Budget of the Federation,* 1981.

An increase in economic activity was forced by means of public expenditure policies producing inordinately high levels of growth. When financial and current account deficits could no longer be financed through domestic and foreign debt, economic activity was deliberately checked. This occurred in 1971 and, to a certain extent, in 1976 and 1977. At the end of the 1970s, oil income was serving to postpone the need to exert such restraints. Until the winter of 1981-1982, the Mexican government resolutely refused to contemplate the possibility of budget restrictions and tax adjustments. The 1981 Expenditure Budget of the Federation made it clear that economic growth would not be severely restrained for the purpose of reducing inflation. Although the budget did not contain growth targets for the year, it did state the objective of keeping growth below the levels attained during the previous year.[25]

In 1980, average crude-oil exports stood at 828,000 b/d. As this average was increased to 1,225 million b/d in 1981, foreign exchange equal to $16 billion would have been earned by the end of the year (excluding natural-gas exports proceeds) if international oil prices had not fallen during the summer. By the close of President Lopez Portillo's six-year term of office, total foreign earnings during the 1980-1982 period would have stood at approximately $50 billion (official calculations using 1.5 million b/d in 1982 and an average price of $40 per barrel). If exports were restricted to 1.1 million b/d at a more conservative price, as estimated in the 1980 Global Development Plan, earnings during the period specified would have amounted to $40 billion. These estimates of oil proceeds implied that the state would enjoy a greater expenditure capacity than that anticipated in 1979 and 1980, at the cost of exacerbating inflationary pressures. All these calculations proved inaccurate in mid-1981 with the decline of international demand for oil and the worldwide fall in crude prices. Because economic growth was financed not only with oil proceeds but also by heavy external indebtedness, economic growth was abruptly halted within a few months and the prospects of external financial bankruptcy loomed on the horizon.

It is now apparent that the manner in which economic policy was conducted in Mexico during the oil boom of the late 1970s made the objectives of increased employment, expansion of the country's productive capacity, and restraint of inflationary pressures incompatible. It no longer appears feasible in the short and medium term to force the productive capacity to maintain a high rate of growth;[26] instead, either imports will continue to increase indiscriminately and inflation will continue unabated, or severe foreign exchange and imports control will be necessary. The government chose the second option in the fall of 1982 after several partial measures did not bring expected results.

Inflation, with its current magnitude and characteristics, is a relatively new experience for postwar Mexico, just as was the "stagflation" of the mid-1970s. During the 1980s, inflationary pressures may be even greater than those during the 1970s, if the pattern of increasing stagnation and rising prices in the industrialized Western economies over the past years is of any relevance. However, the fact that inflation is a worldwide phenomenon does not mean that Mexico should suffer from greater-than-average price increases if it is recognized that the particular severity of inflation in Mexico is due to domestic development patterns and policies.[27]

The central thrust of present and future Mexican economic policy is to regain reasonable rates of growth without hyper-inflation. Looking at the second part of this problem, a less expansive monetary policy (and a concomitant reduction of the cost of regulated credit) might be appropriate, but it must, of necessity, be combined with a strengthening of basic consumer goods production within the framework of the reduced rate of growth. Otherwise, the aims laid down with regard to social policy in the development plans and programs of the late 1970s must be sacrificed at considerable political and historical cost. From all this, one may conclude that the planning of the 1970s, based upon assumptions no longer viable, now restricts the margin of maneuverability of present governmental policy. If such is the case, its objectives and aims must be revised.

Although during the years to come employment will continue to be the central point of policy (this being of logical and fundamental importance in a labor-surplus developing country), the battle against inflation will have to be stepped up and economic and social policy instruments rethought in order to prevent them from becoming mutually exclusive or contradictory. Combating inflation implies state direction of the economy: first, by its more direct intervention in the fixing of prices, and second, by its closer control of monetary variables, especially the rate of interest. The reprogramming of objectives and instruments must be undertaken in accordance with developments in and prospects for the oil sector. The recent rates of overall growth were the result, first and foremost, of the rate of expansion in the production and export of hydrocarbons. This link between the behavior of the oil sector and economic growth will continue for quite some time. In view of the facts that the Mexican economy is increasingly oriented toward oil and that the rate of inflation is rising, it would not appear extreme to opt for a drop in the rate of hydrocarbon exports, keeping in mind the need for foreign exchange to alleviate the burden of the external debt. To do so would necessitate a rethinking of the role played by the oil sector in the economy and a redefinition of the future implications of oil.

MEDIUM- AND LONG-TERM PLANNING

Perhaps in part because the appearance of Mexican oil in 1977-1978 was an almost complete surprise, the only global plan to have been used at the beginning of the 1980s has been purely circumstantial. In view of the stagnation of the import-substitution model, the future of economic development in Mexico was not entirely clear. The scope of the export-substitution model, which has been put forward by many authors as a possible sequel to import substitution is very limited.[28] Export substitution implies the export of products in which the industrialized economies might lose interest because of the dynamism of their high technology sectors even if they were not in the midst of a deep economic recession. However, this model has not been successfully implemented, even in the case of agricultural products, as is demonstrated by large purchases of grain from the United States.

The need to restructure Mexican export policy has led many experts to put forward even inoperate or regressive solutions. Some propose that the export of all industrial products should be simultaneously promoted since the nature of interindustrial relations is such that it is feasible to increase production in one branch at the same time as in all the others. Although this might appear logical in theory, experience has shown that although Mexico has large surpluses in oil and mining industries, it produces insufficient and noncompetitive steel, cement, and capital goods. The simultaneous increase of exporting capacity in these branches would imply reducing current production in the extraction industries and waiting for other industries to become stronger and competitive (without, however, having sufficient foreign currency available). This process would necessarily extend beyond the end of the century, and it would result in heavy social costs.

The regressive solution is advocated by those who see Hong Kong, South Korea, Singapore, Taiwan, and even Brazil as examples for Mexico to follow. Experts and politicians who advance such a solution admire the exporting capacity of these countries; however, they forget that this capacity is generated in a largely denationalized industrial sector (the first four are instances of assembly work) in which the working class in particular is sacrificed. To adopt a model of this type would imply a resumption of industrial and social practices that Mexico is seeking to eradicate. However, for Mexico the oil industry may constitute a good basis for consolidating the export of products with considerable value added and reasonable profits, without involving the need to denationalize the economy, to export simple manufactured goods with relatively low rates of profit, or to wait for the less dynamic sectors of the economy to grow stronger in order to be in a position to undertake the balanced export of goods of all types. If it is given that the short-term model, in which principally crude oil and natural gas are exported, is already operating, it is important to consider what can be done in this field in the medium and long term. The most viable solution for the near future would appear to be oil-based products and, in the long term, products produced by the primary and secondary petrochemical industry as long as productivity increases assure their competitiveness abroad. As a matter of fact, some are competitive.

The viability of the model in which exports of primary hydrocarbons are replaced by exports of oil-based products and petrochemicals is dependent mainly on political and technological factors whose solution in turn depends on the negotiating power the Mexican state derives from its crude and natural gas reserves availability. It should be clearly understood that until Mexico strengthens its industry of oil-based products and catches up with the industrialized countries in this sphere, it will continue to be forced to sell primary hydrocarbons. Negotiations in this respect should not be restricted solely to governments; there are oil companies such as Gulf, Shell, Exxon, and British Petroleum who could also participate given their experience in all the processes involved in the oil cycle and their need for hydrocarbons, either for resale or for processing. At present, Mexico is in direct or indirect contact with some of these companies. Legislation with respect to foreign investment, past experience in the transfer of technology, and the need to improve on traditional patterns of economic development may prevent a repetition of past mistakes caused by hasty negotiation and the objective of industrialization at any cost.

A plan of this nature must consider three obvious factors: (1) hydrocarbons, the raw material required by the petrochemical and refining industries, are nonrenewable resources; (2) the secondary petrochemical industry is in the hands of private enterprise and the current administration has indicated that the state will become no more than a minority partner;[29] and (3) certain sectors are not confident that markets can be found for oil-based products. There are certain observations that should be made regarding each of these points.

Highly relevant statistics exist with regard to the exhaustion of the raw material. At the beginning of 1981, proven hydrocarbon reserves stood at 60 billion barrels, three-quarters crude oil and one-quarter natural gas.[30] At present rates of exploitation, the reserves would allow approximately 59 years of production for crude oil and 56 years for natural gas. If Mexican exports of both products are maintained at early 1981 levels (approximately 1.1 million b/d of crude oil and 300 million cf/d [cubic feet per day] of natural gas) and if, in the short term, a reduction proposed in the Energy Program could be brought about in the income elasticity of domestic demand for hydrocarbons (1.7 during the 1975-1979 period and expected to drop to between 1.0 and 1.3 during the 1981-1990 period), Mexican proven reserves would last at least until the year 2025. By that time, even without additional proven reserves, Mexico will have spanned the energy gap between hydrocarbons and alternative sources of energy.

If hydrocarbon reserves are to be made to last until 2025, certain changes will have to occur in policy in this field. First, exports of crude oil and natural gas will have to be kept at their present levels and attempts will have to be made to gradually substitute oil-based products for these hydrocarbon exports.[31] Second, the high rate of increase in domestic demand for both products will have to be curbed, implying a radical increase in current prices. It should be borne in mind in this respect that natural gas is the major input in Mexico's petrochemical industry[32] and that this industry's products would be used to strengthen the domestic production structure and the nonoil sector of exports. If this is to be achieved, not only will the state have to strengthen its managing role but consumption patterns for this energy resource will have to be modified, principally by marketing it close to its true value. This is of utmost importance since gas has traditionally been viewed as a free by-product of crude output. In 1977, PEMEX absorbed 39 percent of total natural gas production in combined consumption and wastage. This figure stood at 16 percent for crude oil.[33] Although, by the beginning of 1981, natural gas flaring had been reduced considerably except at offshore fields, implying a reduction in wastage and an increase in consumption, there are many factors that demonstrate the scant importance attributed to this product--as compared to other energy sources, especially crude oil. On the Mexican oil scene, the only products showing a surplus are primary hydrocarbons and oil products, whereas a deficit still exists for petrochemicals (see Table 2.6). This contradiction will have to be rectified as soon as possible in order to make exportable surpluses available in this field in the future.[34]

When Mexico began construction in 1978 of the Cactus-Reynosa gas pipeline, which was to have enabled export to the United States of 2 billion cf/d of natural gas (about 60 percent of the country's consumption), it became apparent that large surpluses of this type of energy existed. When the wells of the Gulf of Campeche became operational, natural gas production increased in spite of the lower gas-to-oil ratio; but at the beginning of 1981, 550 million cf/d were still lost in flaring in that area.[35] Following unfruitful negotiations on the sale of natural gas to the United States, the Mexican government decreed in 1979 that PEMEX and the Federal Commission of Electricity should modify their energy consumption patterns and install a dual system that would allow them to begin to substitute natural gas for liquid fuels. It was calculated at the time that the Federal Commission of

Table 2.6
Oil Balance, 1970-1980 (millions of pesos)

	1970	1971	1972	1973	1974	1975	1976	1977	1978	1979	1980
Exports											
Crude oil	--	--	--	--	773	5,490	6,795	22,707	40,048	87,659	217,335
Oil products	370	339	268	388	775	317	199	524	212	1,555	8,838
Petrochemical products	47	48	35	59	119	54	9	76	1,536	2,476	2,771
Natural gas	87	46	19	4	1	--	--	124	--	--	10,300
Total	504	433	322	451	1,668	5,861	7,003	23,431	41,796	91,690	239,244
Imports											
Crude oil & gas	--	24	401	1,129	994	--	--	--	--	--	--
Oil products	414	860	780	2,177	3,399	2,820	1,757	1,189	3,282	4,799	5,591
Petrochemical products	139	163	235	300	932	712	1,658	3,599	3,722	7,627	12,025
Total	553	1,047	1,416	3,606	5,325	3,532	3,415	4,788	7,004	12,426	17,616
Balance	-49	-614	-1,094	-3,155	-3,657	2,329	3,588	18,643	34,792	79,264	221,628

Sources: Secretaria de Programacion y Presupuesto (Department of Programming and Budgeting), *La industria petrolera en Mexico* (The Oil Industry in Mexico), 1979; PEMEX, *Activities File*, 1979 and 1980.

Electricity alone would absorb 1.1 billion cf/d of gas, that is, 55 percent of the gas that was to have been transported by the Cactus-Reynosa pipeline. It was also hoped that through a policy of subsidized prices, other industries would follow the commission's example. When negotiations with the United States broke down, the pipeline remained unfinished; the compression valves were not installed, thereby reducing its transporting capacity by more than 50 percent. Furthermore, the gas that the United States finally agreed to buy from Mexico (only 15 percent of the volume originally planned) is produced in Tamaulipas and, in order to justify to some extent the existence of the gas pipeline, it was agreed that gas would be sold to industries in northern Mexico at subsidized prices.

The Energy Program recognized the possibility that at given times natural gas production could exceed domestic consumption and exports. The best solution would be to use this gas, and even some of the gas that is sold at subsidized prices, to strengthen the primary petrochemical industry. The high level of production of heavy oil in the Gulf of Campeche (and later in Chicontepec, if and when this area goes into production) will make available sufficient fuel that is highly priced abroad. Therefore, the volumes of natural gas currently viewed as surpluses will cease to be the "Trojan horse" of low prices. They will further allow the national oil industry to expand horizontally and, through the primary petrochemical industry, begin to produce goods with greater value added.

Of course, in the case of secondary petrochemicals, a further consideration arises with respect to the system here proposed since many observers have doubts as to the effectiveness of state action in this sector. It is time to change the passive state attitude of the past. If agreements and alliances do not produce concrete results, then it is up to the state to intervene directly. It possesses some of the principal instruments required to do so. Among the secondary petrochemical activities that could be of interest to the state, there are some with very high profit levels and others of great importance to social welfare. Among the activities of interest are the production of synthetic foodstuffs, pharmaceutical products, synthetic fiber clothing, and others, such as plastics, cosmetics, soap, detergent, industrial resins, and polyethylene products.[36]

A few arguments discounting fears that markets do not exist for oil-based products are as follows. As far as refined products are concerned, large volumes of oil products are sold daily in other than contract operations on the world's spot markets (generally at below official prices) of, for instance, Rotterdam, Italy, or the Gulf in the Middle East.[37] In spite of the constant criticism that OPEC member countries do not include added value in their oil, they export 38 percent of the oil-based products sold in the world as a whole.[38] And as for the petrochemical industry, one would assume that markets exist throughout the world; Mexico, for example, which processes the raw material in sufficient volumes, is nonetheless a net importer of some oil-based products.

The implementation of an export-substitution plan such as the one here advanced could constitute the most significant decision in the sphere of oil policy to be taken during this decade. A logical point of departure would be a revision of the pattern of resource allocation. The considerable proportion of public expenditure absorbed by PEMEX for ongoing activities and expansion is a well-known fact. A major portion of this expenditure has been channeled toward exploration and exploitation programs.[39] This allocation of resources may hinder necessary development of refining activities, especially in the field of petrochemicals, and make it very difficult to introduce any changes in the basic hydrocarbon export-oriented industrial oil complex. Corrective action must be taken, first, because of the high opportunity cost involved in idle installed capacity and, second, because investment in the petrochemical industry takes several years to mature (anything between five and ten years, depending on the availability of financial, technological, and human resources)--1982 would have been a rather late date to take a decision to redirect oil policy.[40]

It is vital that the direction in which the oil industry moves be corrected, even if this means failing to reach some of the aims set down in past development plans and programs. Certain investment projects that were previously attributed priority importance might have to be postponed. The redirection further calls for a strengthening of the iron and steel industry (to produce pipes of varying diameter), as well as ports, transport, and other industries. However, it calls above all for political determination. One should go back to the global objectives of the national oil industry, set down by the Director General of PEMEX in 1977 in the following terms: "Today it would be suicide not to export crudes when we are in a position to do so and to wait until we produce petrochemicals which we will never be able to do because, while we do not export crude, we cannot import capital equipment. . . . But we will export crude now in order not to have to do so in the future and be able to export oil-based products instead."[41]

CONCLUSIONS

The reduction of the large proportion of primary hydrocarbons in total exports and their gradual substitution by oil-based products should be considered a basic requirement of oil policy in the years to come. Furthermore, the Mexican state should cease to remain divorced from the secondary petrochemical industry. The results of this latter policy will not become apparent as early as those in the field of hydrocarbon exports but will last longer and present greater possibilities for radically reformulating the traditional import-substitution model. The main advantages to be derived from this policy are:

1. Nonoil exports will increase through the strengthening and greater competitiveness of the refining and the primary and secondary petrochemical industries. This will attenuate the current mono-exporting nature of the Mexican economy.
2. It will be possible to alleviate certain bottlenecks that currently exist.
3. Sustained and less dependent economic development will be ensured until at least the first quarter of the next century.
4. The latent fear that hydrocarbons will be replaced by other sources of energy, causing them to lose their value as primary fuels, will eradicate hydrocarbon wastage.
5. As a company, PEMEX will develop its horizontal expansion capacity, something which the world's most dynamic oil companies have already achieved.
6. The state will strengthen its directing role in the domestic economy by extending its range of activity into new branches of production and will perhaps realize in full its oil wealth-based negotiating power with other countries.

NOTES

The author thanks Carlos Abalo, Carlos de Llano, Oscar Guzman, and Marcela Serrato for their helpful comments.

1. A classic paper on this subject has been written by Maria Concepcion Tavares, "El proceso de sustitucion de importaciones como modelo de desarrollo reciente en America Latina" (The import substitution process as a recent model of development in Latin America), *Boletin Economico de America Latina,* No. 1, United Nations, New York, 1974.

2. On this subject, see the paper by Miguel S. Wionczek, "El crecimiento Latinoamericano y las estrategias de comercio internacional en la posguerra" (Postwar Latin American growth and trade strategies), *Lecturas,* No. 16, Fondo de Cultura Economica, Mexico, not dated. In this essay, the author recalls that (1) import substitution in Latin America dates back to the end of the nineteenth century; (2) the drive toward industrialization in the region occurred during World War I, the

great depression, and World War II; (3) from 1945 onward, world demand increased relatively more slowly; and (4) import substitution does not follow chronological order in all countries of the region.

3. It is not within the scope of this chapter to identify individually the branches of industrial production in which the rate of import substitution came to a standstill or regressed during the 1970s. One of the most outstanding was that of metals. The share of national supply in meeting demand may be measured branch by branch in the figures published in *Producto Interno Bruto y Gasto 1970-1979* (Gross Domestic Product and Expenditure) by the Banco de Mexico. Calculations made by the Mexican Economy Department of the CIDE (Center of Demographic and Economic Research) appear in *Economia Mexicana,* No. 2, 1980.

4. For many years CEPAL maintained that Latin America would conclude all phases of the import-substitution process by the end of the 1960s at the latest. See Raul Prebisch, *Transformacion y Desarrollo* (Transformation and Development), Fondo de Cultura Economica, Mexico, 1971.

5. The first few years of direct foreign investment in Mexico showed a positive balance which, however, later became negative. In 1970, the payments ratio of such investment (purchase of goods and services and contracting of loans) stood at 2.24 since payments were on the order of $882.1 million and income was about $364.1 million. In 1977 the ratio reached 3.69 (payments of $1,772.6 million against investment income of $318.2 million) according to figures issued by the Banco de Mexico.

6. See Arturo Huerta, *El modelo de desarrollo economico reciente en Mexico* (The model of recent economic development in Mexico), thesis, Nuevo Leon University, 1974.

7. Calculated on the basis of figures contained in the annual reports of the Banco de Mexico and in its *Producto Interno Bruto y Gasto 1970-1979* (Gross Domestic Product and Expenditure).

8. Further disadvantages of losing control of the economy are contained in Donald B. Keesing, "El financiamiento externo y los requerimientos de plena modernizacion en Mexico" (Foreign financing and requirements of full modernization in Mexico), *Foro Internacional,* No. 61, El Colegio de Mexico, July-September 1975, p. 4.

9. The speed with which oil potential in the Gulf of Campeche was developed demonstrates the degree to which this is viable in the short term.

10. See World Bank, *Special Study of the Mexican Economy: Major Policy Issues and Prospects, 1977-1982,* Washington, D.C., December 1978. The liberalism of Mexican foreign trade caused imports of consumer goods to increase by 80 percent in 1979 and by 142 percent in 1980, which is, of course, considerably higher than for other imported goods. See Banco de Mexico, *Annual Report,* 1980 (preliminary), p. 85.

11. David Ibarra Munoz, *Proyecto de Ley de Ingresos de*

la Federacion (Draft of the Federation Income Law), 1981, p. VII.

12. For a review of foreign trade in the agricultural sector over the past few years, see "La balanza comercial de productos agricolas" (The trade balance of agricultural products), in *Comercio Exterior,* Vol. 30, No. 7 (July 1980), p. 689.

13. Mexico's international monetary reserves, including gold and silver, stood at US$1,411 million at the end of 1976; by the end of 1979, they had reached US$3,088 million. Hence they changed from 0.6 percent to 0.8 percent of the world total during that period. Banco de Mexico, *Boletin de Indicadores Economicos Internacionales* (Bulletin of International Economic Indicators), July-September 1980.

14. Of course the possibility of oil squandering should not be excluded. This occurs principally through luxury consumption, although ostentatious investment may also occur (unnecessary roads, nonpriority buildings, etc.). Neither can it be ruled out that, in the manner of other hydrocarbon-exporting countries, Mexico might fall back on what is in some circles called the "oil resource safety belt," consisting of investment abroad by banks. This would be an extreme measure since crude price increases have shown that it is preferable to keep oil resources underground rather than to sell them and deposit the currency thus earned in foreign banks. Temporary drops in oil exports may also occur and international crude prices may fall, but not to a degree sufficient to cancel the long-term trend.

15. It must, however, be recognized that the problem of foreign indebtedness is still very serious. Mexico is a developing country and has the world's largest foreign debt after Brazil, and the solvency coefficient (payments for servicing of the debt/total exports of goods and services) is very high: 0.36 in 1976 and 0.62 in 1979. Banco de Mexico, *Annual Report,* various issues.

16. David Ibarra Munoz, op. cit., p. 3.

17. The model that takes 27 percent as the optimal level for the domestic savings/GDP coefficient may be found in Rene Villarreal, "El petroleo como instrumento de desarrollo y de negociacion internacional: Mexico en los ochentas" (Oil as an instrument of development and international negotiation: Mexico during the eighties), *El Trimestre Economico,* No. 189 (January-March 1981).

18. It was established in the Energy Program that growth could reach 8 percent annually during the 1980s without exporting in excess of 1.5 million b/d of crude oil and 300 million cf/d of natural gas. However, it was also pointed out that, for technical reasons, maximum oil and gas production could at no time exceed 8 to 10 million b/d of crude-oil equivalent. If for some reason this level of production was reached, greater surpluses than anticipated would be available for export.

19. If Mexico experienced serious problems related to foreign currency absorption and inflation with export levels of 828,000 b/d of oil in 1979, one might ask what would happen if projected exports of 1.5 million b/d were reached in 1981, assuming the price remained high, i.e., 81 percent more than in 1980. This is considerably higher than the average annual growth rate of 54.5 percent registered between 1975 and 1980.

20. During each month of 1980, oil exports remained below 1 million b/d except during September and October when they reached the 1 million b/d mark. Department of Interior, General Office of Customs.

21. However gradual, the policy of opening foreign trade is conflictive. Observers of various sectors suggest that previous import permits be maintained and reject the efficacy of import tariffs. They consider that the stagnation of certain branches and sectors of the economy in import substitution results from decreased protectionism. See SEPAFIN, *Industria manufacturera: efectos de la neuva politica de comercio exterior* (The manufacturing industry: effects of new foreign trade policy), mimeo., Mexico, 1980.

22. The absence until a few years ago of scientific and technological planning and the need for technical and scientific personnel and trained labor led Mexico's education and labor authorities to recognize that it will be necessary in the short term to import technical experts to maintain the present rate of economic growth and that efforts to train labor will have to be redoubled to ensure that the rate of training keeps pace with the country's needs. This, in conjunction with the problems set forth at the beginning of this chapter in developing or adapting imported technology to the needs of Mexico, led the authorities of the 1978-1982 National Science and Technology Program to suggest that national expenditure in this field be increased from 0.61 percent of GDP in 1978 to 1 percent by 1982.

23. Mexico is a country of predominantly young people: of every four individuals, one works and supports the other three. Hence, job sources in the future should be labor intensive.

24. Although the social implications of the Ley de Fomento Agropecuario (Law of Agricultural Development) will not be examined in this chapter, they are nonetheless of considerable importance.

25. *Proyecto de Ley de Ingresos de la Federacion*, op. cit., pp. XXIII, XXXI, XXXII. However, should income from oil not reach projected levels, expenditure could be reduced, causing a drop in the growth of GDP. See note 14, *supra.*

26. On this subject, a U.S. newspaper reported that the government is attempting to activate its oil economy at an annual growth rate of 8 percent although its natural growth rate is lower. Mexico should not seek to achieve a rate of economic expansion above the rate of 6.5 percent: Alan Robinson, "Inflation Could Dash Mexican Oil Hopes,"

The Journal of Commerce, January 16, 1981.

27. Over recent years, prices to the consumer in Mexico have increased much more rapidly than in the countries with which it has closest trade links. With a base 100 for the whole world in 1975, the Mexican price index had reached 265.6 in 1980 while it stood at 152.9 in the United States, 122.6 in the Federal Republic of Germany, 138.1 in Japan, 230 in Spain, 165.2 in France, and 171.4 in Venezuela. See Banco de Mexico, *Boletin de Indicadores Economicos Internacionales*, op. cit. The same may be said of the rate of interest paid by Mexico to international creditors. The preferential interest and repayment conditions attached to Mexico's latest loans are well known.

28. For an introduction to the export-substitution model and its possible application in Mexico, see Rene Villarreal, "Del proyecto de credimiento y sustitucion de exportaciones" (From the project of growth and import substitution to the project of development and export substitution), *Comercio Exterior*, Vol. 25, No. 3 (March 1975).

29. Jorge Diaz Serrano, *Informe del Director General de PEMEX* (Report of the Director General of PEMEX), PEMEX, Mexico, March 1978, p. 15.

30. Jose Lopez Portillo, *Cuarto Informe de Govierno 1980* (Fourth Government Report 1980); and SEPAFIN, *Programa de Energia: Metas a 1990 y proyecciones al ano 2000* (Energy Program: Targets for 1990 and forecasts for the year 2000), 1980.

31. The Energy Program bears witness to the possibility of having sizeable surpluses of oil-based products in the short term, in view of the fact that current PEMEX programs establish that the level of production in this area would be adequate until 1984 and forecast that priority will be given to the production of gasoline and kerosenes, these being the oil-based products fetching the highest prices abroad.

32. Natural gas makes up 65 percent of the inputs of the primary petrochemical industry, and the remainder consists of liquid hydrocarbons. The price of natural gas for domestic consumption is approximately ten times lower than its export price and the ratio is similar for liquid hydrocarbons due, first and foremost, to the fact that international prices rise far more rapidly than domestic prices and, second, that the United States, which defines a large part of world energy policy, has decreed that oil prices will be definitively freed at the beginning and not at the end of 1981, as specified in U.S. President Jimmy Carter's second energy plan. Again, prices constitute the primary reason why natural gas consumption in Mexico has risen by 23 percent whereas consumption of oil-based products rose by only 15 percent.

33. Jaime Corredor, "Oil in Mexico," Oxford Energy Seminar, 1980, Table 48 of mimeographed paper.

34. If this is to be achieved, major changes must be made in oil policy, since until now its objectives have revolved around hydrocarbons production. This is

demonstrated by the fact that, while crude oil production more than quadrupled between 1976 and 1980, the volume of oil-based products increased by only 56 percent and that of primary petrochemicals by 83 percent during the same period. See the figures presented by the Director General of PEMEX in his *Informe de Labores* (Report of activities) of March 18, 1981.

35. Jorge Diaz Serrano (Director General of PEMEX) *Informe Anual* (Annual report), 1980.

36. To appreciate fully the great impact of hydrocarbons on the economy, see the behavior of terms of trade of the oil industry by sectors in PEMEX and the Department of Programming and Budgeting, "La industria petrolera en Mexico" (The oil industry in Mexico), 1980, Table 11.89.

37. In order to appreciate the extent of sales of oil-based products in these markets, see tables on the subject appearing in the weekly *Petroleum Intelligence Weekly* (New York).

38. Figures corresponding to 1978, Organization of the Petroleum Exporting Countries (OPEC), *Annual Report*, Vienna, Austria, 1978.

39. In PEMEX's 1980 expenditure budget, exploration and exploitation programs account for a total of 170,429.8 million Mexican pesos whereas those related to refining and petrochemical production stand at barely 41,704.7 million pesos; see Secretaria de Programacin y Presupuesto, *Presupuesto de Egrosos de la Federacion 1980* (Department of Programming and Budgeting, Federal Expenditure Budget, 1980).

40. Although it is possible that by the end of 1981 the primary petrochemical industry could indeed show a surplus, as stated by the Director General of PEMEX (*Informe de Labores*, March 1981), the real development of primary and secondary petrochemical exports will take longer.

41. *Tiempo*, Mexico, March 21, 1977.

3
New Energy Sources in Mexico: The Present Situation and Prospects for the Future

Oscar M. Guzman

The development of "new" energy sources[1] in Mexico is a relatively recent occurrence, dating from the second half of the 1970s. A massive diffusion of systems and techniques that would permit using the different nonconventional energy sources has not yet taken place, and, consequently, the proportion of these energy resources in total energy supply is insignificant. For instance, some energy is generated from geothermal reserves. Since its first use in the 1950s, this type of energy now represents almost 2 percent of total electricity generation. However, despite their great potential, geothermal and other nonconventional energy sources have not challenged the primacy of hydrocarbons. Although the country has one of the world's largest geothermal deposits, a high level of exposure to the sun's energy,[2] and an extensive sea coast and although its sizeable agricultural production provides sufficient resources for the production of biomass energy, small- and medium-scale electric power generation capacity has not been developed to any extent.

A comparison of the sources of energy reserves reveals the importance of geothermal resources in the context of Mexico's total energy reserves position (Table 3.1). In conventional terms, the outlook for the country's energy potential is dominated by crude oil and natural gas, which constitute 85.7 percent of both proven and probable energy reserves. Although proven geothermal reserves make up barely 0.6 percent of total reserves, the percentage changes substantially when probable and potential reserves are considered. In fact, probable geothermal reserves exceed uranium resources, and potential geothermal reserves rank as the second largest source of energy after liquid and gaseous hydrocarbons. Despite the uncertainty inherent in delineating potential reserves, preliminary evaluations have indicated that geothermal resources account for 15 percent of total potential energy reserves in the country.

Table 3.1
Mexico's Energy Reserves

	Crude Oil (a)	Natural Gas (b)	Subtotal (a) + (b)	Coal	Hydraulic	Uranium	Geothermal	Total
In Millions of TOE (tons of oil equivalent)								
Proven	6,808	3,387	10,195	856	638	130	74	11,893
Probable	--	--	18,500	1,000	1,356	260	484	21,600
Potential	--	--	35,397	1,419	3,988	1,300	7,440	49,544
As Percent of Total Reserves								
Proven	66.8*	33.2*	85.7	7.2	5.4	1.1	0.6	100
Probable	--	--	85.7	4.6	6.3	1.3	2.2	100
Potential	--	--	71.4	3.0	8.0	3.1	15.0	100

*Percentage of subtotal

Notes: Natural gas: includes nonassociated gas and gas liquids. *Coal:* figures given are for in situ reserves, evaluated according to the caloric content of coal. *Hydraulic:* reserves estimated in accordance with the consumption of oil products by an equivalent thermal power station operating for thirty years. Potential reserves were evaluated in terms of the country's theoretical gross hydroelectricity potential. *Uranium:* the energy that could be generated per unit of uranium consumed was calculated and then the consumption of oil products by an equivalent thermal power station was estimated. *Geothermal: Proven* included high enthalpy, water and steam reserves; *probable* includes high, medium, and low enthalpy reserves; *potential* includes super hot water, steam geo-pressurized and lava reserves.

Sources: Petroleos Mexicanos, the Federal Electricity Commission, the Ministry of Resources and Industrial Development, and the Geothermal Department of the Institute of Electricity Research.

RESEARCH AND DEVELOPMENT OF ENERGY RESOURCES

Responsibility for the development of Mexico's impressive endowment of reserves rests with various institutes and centers, and their nature forms the character of the initial progress made in this area. Seventy percent are institutes or centers dedicated to teaching and research. Another 20 percent are independent associations, and the remaining 10 percent are centralized or decentralized government bodies. In most of the university-affiliated institutes and centers, teaching is the main activity; research, without being unimportant, is given lower priority and is seen as complementary to teaching.

Research and development constitute the main work of the centers. Almost 70 percent of the projects involve primary sources of energy, 20 percent relate to technical research, and only 10 percent involve dissemination of the results. The diffusion of the uses of new energy sources is not divorced from research and development activities: attempts to diffuse the know-how form part of designing, constructing, and operating experimental units by the different groups, all seeking to expand the market for the various types of technology.

An increasing use of manpower can be observed in the development of new sources of energy in Mexico. The figure of 1,541 man-months worked in 1979 rose to 1,755 in 1980 and to approximately 1,888 by 1982, representing increases of 14 percent and 6.8 percent, respectively. A breakdown of the distribution of labor in new energy sources development reveals a slight shift in the priority of the different sources of nonconventional energy (see Tables 3.2 and 3.3).

Total funding received by the centers reached $6.8 million in 1980 and went up by 43 percent in 1981 to $9.8 million.[3] Resources set aside for new energy sources in 1982 were more than double those of the previous year and totaled almost $22 million (Table 3.4). Whether funding continued to increase during the present financial crisis cannot be ascertained.

In the first three years (1979-1981) for which figures are given in Table 3.5, the accumulated financing assigned to new energy sources' research and development totaled about $9 million. Increasing at an annual rate of approximately 24 percent from 1979 to 1981, financing for 1981 reached $3.6 million and is expected to total $4.6 million in 1982.

In the period mentioned, 72 percent of the financing received by the different organizations and centers originated in domestic expenditure but not necessarily from credit institutions. Resources granted to the centers, in addition to their budgets, from domestic sources during that period totaled $6.4 million; of this, $4 million, or 45 percent of total financing for these activities, was provided by the Mexican federal government. Of the

Table 3.2
Distribution of Human Resources among New Energy Sources Development

	Solar							
	Photothermic Conversion	Photovoltaic Conversion	Total for Solar	Geothermal	Biomass and Others	Wind	Wave	Total
1980	45.6	21.8	67.4	24.6	4.3	3.2	0.5	100
1981	44.0	21.7	65.7	27.1	4.0	2.8	0.4	100
1982	41.6	25.0	66.6	25.1	5.2	2.7	0.4	100

Sources: Petroleos Mexicanos, the Federal Electricity Commission, the Ministry of Resources and Industrial Development, and the Geothermal Department of the Institute of Electricity Research.

Table 3.3
Manpower Employed in Work on New Energy Sources by Main Categories, 1981 (percentage of total employed manpower)

	Solar				
	Photothermal Conversion	Photovoltaic Conversion	Geothermal	Biomass and Others	Wind
Management and highly qualified professionals	60.6	71.0	63.5	52.0	44.0
Medium-level professionals and qualified technical staff	25.7	24.0	26.0	46.9	37.0
Other	13.7	5.0	10.5	1.1	19.0

Sources: Petroleos Mexicanos, the Federal Electricity Commission, the Ministry of Resources and Industrial Development, and the Geothermal Department of the Institute of Electricity Research.

Table 3.4
Distribution of Economic Resources Among New Energy Sources (percentage and millions of dollars)

	Solar				Biomass and Others	Wind	Wave	Total	
	Photothermal Conversion	Photovoltaic Conversion	Total for Solar	Geothermal				Percent	Dollars
1980	51.9	14.1	66.0	28.5	2.7	2.5	0.3	100	6.8623
1981	55.0	16.0	71.0	23.2	3.9	3.9	0.1	100	9.8245
1982	77.2	7.2	84.4	13.2	1.9	1.6	0.1	100	21.8673

Sources: Petroleos Mexicanos, the Federal Electricity Commission, the Ministry of Resources and Industrial Development, and the Geothermal Department of the Institute of Electricity Research.

Table 3.5
Extrabudgetary Financing of Work on New Sources in Relation to Total Financing Available

	Total Financing Resources (in millions of dollars)	Extrabudgetary Financing (in millions of dollars)	Percent+
1979	--	2.387	--
1980	6.862	2.963	43.2
1981	9.824	3.644	37.0
1982*	21.867	4.613**	21.0

*Estimated amount according to forecasts made by the centers

**If expected credits equivalent to $1.29 million awarded, this total would increase to $5.9 million.

+Percentages may not equal 100 due to rounding.

Sources: Petroleos Mexicanos, the Federal Electircity Commission, the Ministry of Resources and Industrial Development, and the Geothermal Department of the Institute of Electricity Research.

$9 million assigned to the centers between 1979 and 1981, just three centers received 83.3 percent of the total and the other three only 5 percent each.

ALTERNATIVE ENERGY SOURCES: POTENTIAL AND POLICY

Despite the magnitude of Mexico's energy sources--including nonconventional ones--almost a third of the total population (20 million people) are without electricity, and a large part of the population as a whole underconsumes energy. The lowest income city dwellers, and, above all, inhabitants of the country's marginal rural areas, make up the sectors most affected by the lack of energy supplies. The development of alternative energy sources could contribute to meeting part of the needs of the rural population, particularly in regions where human settlements are very scattered and highly isolated from the larger population centers. An integrated combination of processes using solar, biomass, and, in some cases, wind energy and energy from streams and small waterfalls would constitute an energy alternative for these backward areas. The development of new energy sources is not only possible and desirable, but also vital both to improve the quality of life and the methods employed in production and, as a corollary, to stem trends of rural-urban migration that are caused mainly by the deterioration of the peasants' economic situation.

New energy sources can not only provide a solution to the energy consumption and production needs of the rural population but can also contribute to a more rational use of energy in the residential and industrial areas of the country. Solar architectural design, on the one hand, and the generation of medium- and low-temperature steam, on the other, are areas in which the use of solar energy would encourage a savings in conventional fuels. Progress in these areas would affect the sectoral energy balance and redress the environmental pollution that has reached critical levels in some cities. Thus, there are many justifiable reasons for developing new energy sources in the country.

The official guidelines governing energy policy explicitly suggest the appropriateness of nonconventional sources.[4] Various governmental organizations are taking part in particular projects, with the federal government providing the main financing for studies of the energy resources. However, an overall national program for the development of these sources has yet to be formulated, much less to be implemented. Such a program would have to be based on an exhaustive analysis of the resources and fields in which immediate action could be taken, using foreign technology adapted to local conditions or developed in the country itself. The overall program would have to establish priorities in this field and coordinate work carried out in the spheres of research, development, production, and diffusion of results. In addition, a tax policy should be conceived and implemented to encourage the production, marketing, and use of conversion equipment for which the initial and operating costs may compare unfavorably with those for conventional heavily subsidized energies.

The lack of a general policy for the promotion of new energy sources (which would include a strategy for diffusing information about these sources in rural areas), together with the extremely low level of industrialization of the existing processes despite a present technological sophistication, consort to limit the extent of usage of new energy sources. Consequently, it is impossible to foresee that these sources will make any significant contribution to diversifying energy supply in the short or medium term. In the long term, their contribution will depend on the financial resources available for their nationwide diffusion.

Currently, the development of new energy sources is jeopardized by the increased domestic availability of hydrocarbons (due to export difficulties) and the financial crisis, which has led to general cutbacks in the budgets of the various institutions. If, in these circumstances, the state reduces its support for ongoing projects, the emergence of these new energy sources and their application to the needs of a vast sector of the country's population would be postponed further, the scientific and technological gap in the energy field between Mexico and the advanced industrial countries would widen, and a new area of foreign dependency would emerge. Moreover, in view of the fact that the development of new energy sources is incipient, future feasibility will basically depend not so much on the free play of market forces as on governmental policies and resources. If new sources are going to prove viable, they will need the same type of financing that other energy sources, and particularly nuclear energy, have required.

Allocation of Manpower

Since work on nonconventional energy sources first started, manpower working in the different areas has expanded continuously. This trend should continue in the immediate future in line with projects underway and those in the planning stage. The labor force devoted to the development of the particular nonconventional energy sources may be construed as evidence of their relative priority and potential practicability.

The labor force employed in photothermic conversion of solar energy is considerably larger than that working on both photovoltaic conversion and projects related to other sources. Work carried out on uses of geothermal energy should be considered separately, because it alone absorbs more human resources than all the other activities put together. There are considerably fewer personnel working on biomass, wind, and wave energy than on solar and geothermal energy.

Manpower is concentrated not just on work on solar and geothermal energy sources but also in a small number of institutes that have attained a high level of specialization. The work they carry out mainly involves basic and applied research, with very little attention being paid to widely diffusing information about conversion equipment.

The majority of people employed in work on the new energy sources fall under the category of highly qualified and medium-level professionals (Table 3.3), reflecting the emphasis on research and the construction of experimental plants. The relatively sound training of professionals in Mexico has made it possible to attain good standards of scientific and technological achievement in this field in a fairly short time.

Allocation of Finances

The increase in the work force employed in the various activities in the recent past was made possible by increased financing devoted to work on new energy sources. Expectations of increased financing pervaded all centers and research institutes prior to the 1982 financial crisis. A larger proportion of spending had been allocated in the past to photothermal conversion of solar energy than to other sources, and this trend was expected to continue. The estimates of financial resources did not include geothermal electric power stations whose annual operating costs are nine or ten times higher than the spending assigned to other nonconventional energy sources, including geothermal research and development projects.

The financial resources for photothermal purposes were basically absorbed by specific projects such as solar architecture, solar electric power generation, and integrated solar projects for agricultural uses. Total spending was not distributed more or less equally among existing centers but was assigned, in the main, to a small number of institutions. A major recipient is a government agency involved in work on integrated solar projects.

The distribution of financial resources among the different energy sources reflects and magnifies the differences revealed in the distribution of manpower. In fact, a proportion of total spending smaller even than the proportion of manpower is assigned to biomass, wind, and wave energy research, confirming the low level of interest that has been aroused in these fields.

Technological Resources

The technological resources employed in work on new energy sources can be divided into two major categories according to the characteristics and size of the centers involved. On the one hand, there is a group of centers that only carry out projects relating to processes using relatively simple technology and not requiring very complex support. Here, often all that is needed is a small mechanical workshop and a few measuring instruments. On the other hand, there is a fairly small group of centers with workshops and laboratories using high-precision equipment, which sometimes includes computer systems, in which not only basic research is carried out but also prototypes are designed and constructed. This polarization of the technological resources available to make advances in new energy sources projects is closely linked to the high concentration of financial resources in a few centers.

Despite this disparity, the scientific and technological capacity has now been acquired, in general, to develop practically all the processes for utilizing the nonconventional sources of energy on which research has been carried out. This is particularly true in the case of design and construction of systems for capturing solar energy, biodigestors, solar housing architecture, and, to a large extent, solar electric power stations. Much less progress has been achieved in the case of photovoltaic cells.

The projects presently implemented, with a few exceptions, have a low specific energy output and can be carried out on a small scale. Whether utilizing simple, intermediate, or complex technologies, there have been no serious obstacles to the diffusion of information about the new energy sources because of the progress that has been achieved in adapting and developing technology to build the systems needed to utilize these sources.

Present scientific and technological capacity would seem to have outstripped industrial demand for producing equipment. However, this appraisal should not lead to the erroneous view that the resources assigned to nonconventional sources of energy in Mexico are more than sufficient to ensure their development and wide use. One can only evaluate whether sufficient resources are set aside for these activities by examining the objectives thought to be reached. Future targets have not yet been defined, but if the different types of new energy sources with their specific features and particular fields of application are to contribute, in accordance with their distinct potentials, to both diversifying the country's energy supply base and introducing new patterns of energy consumption, then it can be argued not only that the resources set aside for these activities are insufficient, but also that their distribution is unsuitable.

An increased usage of energy systems based on new nonconventional sources is partially inhibited by the low level of industrialization, and, therefore, the absence of channels for the marketing of the processes. As yet, there has been no transfer of the technological advances achieved in the research and development phase to industry, which could mass produce the equipment. In some cases, production and marketing costs are factors that contribute to making the equipment less competitive than that for systems using conventional energy sources. Other factors compound this situation: first, the lack of a policy that includes consideration of how to implement the incentives needed to reverse the present situation, and, second, the inevitable distrust by consumers of these simple systems, about which, moreover, they know very little.

Because isolated rural communities, and the rural population in general, should be the main beneficiaries of the use of new energy technologies, it is essential that peasant communities directly participate in the decision making and implementation of projects in this field. Any publicity campaign that is not based on the rural communities' potential for action and that neither matches research and development with the real requirements and resources of these communities in the various regions of the country nor is incorporated into an integrated rural development program will run the serious risk of failure met by earlier experiments.

Additional Financing

The current financial resources of new energy centers and institutes are sometimes augmented by financing from a variety of institutions. This additional financing is a crucial contribution to the realization of the projects designed by the centers; without it, many projects would never get off the ground because as a rule the cost of the projects is larger than the financing initially available. Almost two-thirds of the institutes receive extrabudgetary financing, which most probably will tend to increase in the future.

Financing, which represents some 40 percent of economic resources of the centers, comes mainly from the federal government through the appropriations from the ministerial budgets. Thus, almost all new nonconventional energy activities in Mexico are carried out on the basis of government support that takes the form of either economic resources directly assigned to the centers or financial assistance given to particular projects.

The distribution of financial assistance shares the characteristics of the distribution of economic resources and manpower. Most financing is assigned, on the one hand, to solar energy, and, on the other, to a small number of institutes. This fact restricts the possibilities of more widely developing other sources, particularly wind and wave energy, and retards the implementation of projects in centers with small budgets and little or no access to external sources of financing.

Regional and international organizations have provided financial assistance for the centers, but to a much lesser extent than has the Mexican government. However, their assistance has been used to promote applications of wind and biomass energy, which have suffered differing degrees of neglect. Financial assistance for projects carried out jointly between centers in Mexico and other countries is hindered by the complex requirements needed to obtain money and the slowness of the negotiating process. These factors form an additional obstacle to the development of international cooperation, in general, and to cooperation with the other countries of Latin America, in particular.

Cooperation

Although cooperation between centers throughout the country has increased in recent years, this cooperation is neither formal nor continuous. Links are mainly established between members of the different groups, without recourse to institutional channels, and are based on exchanges of technical information and participation in conferences and seminars. The isolated nature of the programs makes coordination and joint work difficult and in some cases leads to duplication of projects.

The links established by Mexican institutes with similar bodies in other countries form an important part of the overall network of information exchange. Here two unequal types of information flows have developed: the first, and most important, is a flow from the advanced industrial countries to Mexico, and the second, from Mexico to other parts of Latin America. Information exchanges between countries in Latin America are channeled through the Latin American Energy Organization (OLADE), which plays an important role in consolidating relations between centers in the region. The main energy resources on which cooperation between Mexico and Latin America, in particular Central America and the Caribbean, has been concentrated are those of geothermal and biomass energy. Paradoxically, there has been no significant degree of cooperation between Mexico and other countries in the field of solar energy. Recently, efforts have begun to design joint projects for photovoltaic conversion, but as yet no definite agreements have been reached.

The Mexican centers are highly interested in establishing links with the rest of Latin America. The experience of cooperation with OLADE has served to encourage international cooperation. The latter would appear to be a necessity when we consider the relative technological backwardness of the member countries as a whole and their lack of economic resources. The leaders of the Mexican alternative energy research and development centers emphasize the need for international cooperation since, through the latter, similar problems can be dealt with by countries that are not separated by the socioeconomic and cultural gulf existing between them and the advanced industrial nations. The existence of common interests--the fairly similar levels of development, the need to meet the unsatisfied energy demands of wide sectors of the rural population, and the availability of comparable and compatible infrastructural equipment--is a factor that may facilitate an increase in cooperation for a number of nonconventional energy sources, and among a larger number of countries and activities.

PRELIMINARY OUTLINE OF DEVELOPMENT POLICY

The low level of development of new energy sources, in relation to their potential capacity for meeting Mexico's energy needs, suggests it would be advisable to take the following steps.

1. Call a meeting of the directors of the national centers and encourage a detailed discussion of the present situation and future prospects for research and development and mass diffusion of its fruits in the new energy fields. The debate should clarify which problems are currently preventing new sources from being developed, so that the mechanisms needed to promote activities, exchanges, and cooperation may be established.

2. Formulate a development program for new sources of energy, within the framework of overall energy planning in the country. At both levels the new sources should be considered as a real alternative means of meeting the basic energy needs of vast sectors of the population and diversifying energy supply. This program should lay down policy guidelines relating to new energy sources; establish priorities; direct research, development, and production work and the publishing of results; and define a tax incentives policy to promote industrial production, marketing, and use of conversion equipment for new energy sources.

3. Create or identify a national organization that would direct, coordinate, and promote research and development activities concerning new sources. This agency would maintain a permanent list of different centers and of past, present, and future research projects and would publicize relevant information. Such a setup would facilitate access to scientific and technological results already achieved, avoid any unnecessary duplication of research, and, thus, enable more productive usage of available financial and human resources.

The organization should also take part in allocating domestic and external financial resources and, particularly in the case of the latter, speed up their transfer, thus avoiding unnecessary delays in the projects.

4. Facilitate the consolidation of smaller centers while encouraging the creation of new ones so as to decentralize, in both institutional and geographic terms, work being carried out on new energy sources. In this regard, an adequate supply of economic resources should be guaranteed, so as to modify the way in which these resources are allocated presently.

5. Decide upon and implement the economic, productive, and administrative mechanisms needed to consolidate the large-scale development of new energy sources and generate sustained interaction between industry and research centers. In this way, technological innovation and adaptation would be furthered in the context of joint

work in industrial production and in research and development. Concerning this, a study should be conducted to assess the production capacity of new energy sources, explicitly stating the constraints imposed by the limited availability of human, economic, and financial resources.

6. Given the lack of a precise definition and evaluation of the energy potential of new sources, conduct a study to determine the total reserves of nonconventional energy sources in the country.

7. Analyze the possible applications of new energy sources for consumers in urban and rural areas, on the basis of systems using technology that is either already well known or easily adaptable to conditions in the country.

From an analysis of the present state of exchanges and cooperation between national and foreign centers, it can be concluded that it would be necessary as well to

1. Strengthen and consolidate the already existing regional energy organization (OLADE) and consider the possibility of creating a Latin American center dealing specifically with technical, socioeconomic, legal, and political aspects relating to new energy sources.
2. Encourage exchanges of professionals between the centers to accelerate the training of manpower employed in these areas.
3. Create a Latin American teaching center for new energy sources and encourage experts to meet at regional seminars, conferences, and congresses.
4. Seek suitable mechanisms that would allow an intensive, continuous exchange of information and details concerning advances made in the different areas. In this regard, it is proposed that a Latin American information network of nonconventional energy sources be set up.
5. Define common areas of interest and establish work programs for joint projects to be carried out with participation of several centers so as to harness research and development efforts and avoid unnecessary research duplication.
6. Strive to obtain the financing needed so that joint projects may be carried out and regional centers for each energy source set up. To meet this objective, a regional fund should be created to which the countries of Latin America, the international organizations, the industrial countries, and probably the main oil exporting nations would contribute.

NOTES

1. The concept of "new" energy sources has not been clearly defined by energy specialists, despite the existence of a clear consensus about the sources this classi-

fication should include. In this chapter, the category NS (new sources) was used to include primary sources of energy whose development is incipient and for which, at the world level, the technology either is still at an experimental level or has only recently been developed. It also includes certain sources, the technology for which, although well known, has not yet been developed on a sufficiently wide scale for its contribution to energy supply to be considered important. (It excludes nuclear energy.) It also includes geothermal energy, which may be considered to be at an initial stage of commercial development.

The importance of this heterogeneous set of "new" energy sources for Mexico and all the countries in Latin America lies in their capacity to replace scarce hydrocarbons and to provide energy needed for production in regions that are not incorporated into global energy systems.

The "new" energy sources include solar, wind, biomass, tidal, the thermal gradient of the oceans, wave, hydrogen (obtained by hydrolysis), carbon gasification and liquefaction, bituminous schists and asphaltic sands, combustible cells, and small hydraulic sources.

2. Average isolation--the rate of delivery of all direct solar energy per unit of horizontal surface--in the country is estimated at 2,000 kilowatt-hours per square meter per year.

3. Amounts given in dollars were calculated at the December 1980 rate of 23.3 pesos to the U.S. dollar.

4. Secretaria de Patrimonio y Fomento Industrial, *Programma de Energia: Goals to 1990 and Forecasts to the Year 2000* (Summary and Conclusions) (Mexico: November 1980).

4
Natural Gas in Mexico

Adrian Lajous-Vargas

Mexico is in a unique position among large industrializing countries: its massive energy resource endowment is being developed within the framework of a diversified economic structure with historically high growth rates. From 1950 to 1980, the gross domestic product (GDP) grew at an average annual rate of 6.5 percent. During this period the share of manufactures in nonoil GDP increased from 19 to 25 percent, and the manufacturing sector's share of employment expanded from 12 to 20 percent. More recently the Mexican economy has experienced a very rapid growth due in part to the substantial inflow of oil revenues. In the last four years the GDP has grown at 8.5 percent annually, industry at 9.6 percent, and investment in real terms at 18 percent.

Natural gas use is best understood within the context of manufacturing industry's size and growth. Today, Mexico is the tenth largest market economy (when measured in terms of manufacturing's proportion in GDP). In absolute size Mexico's manufacturing sector is larger than that of Sweden, the Netherlands, Belgium, Denmark, or Norway. Mexican industry is fourteen times larger than that of Singapore, eleven times that of Chile, five times that of South Korea, and twice that of Argentina and India. What is also remarkable in these comparisons is that this level of industrial development has been attained in only three decades.

Natural gas plays a key role in Mexico's energy balance. Between 1977 and 1981, gross production of natural gas doubled, reaching a level of 4 billion cubic feet per day(cf/d) or 42 billion cubic meters (cm). Associated gas represented 75 percent of this total. In 1981 natural gas provided one-fifth of Mexico's total primary energy needs, a share equivalent to that of industrialized countries as a whole. Consumption of this hydrocarbon is concentrated in the manufacturing sector and in the oil industry itself. Last year Petroleos Mexicanos (PEMEX), the national oil company, used 1.2 billion cf/d (13 billion cm) and sold 1.0 billion cf/d (11 billion cm) to industry.

These two figures add up to three-fourths of total net availability. Crucially, 45 percent of the industrial sector's final energy consumption is provided by natural gas. The importance of gas transcends its calorific value: it is difficult to substitute as a source of energy in a wide number of processes, and it is a basic raw material in strategic branches of Mexican industry.

As of March 1982, total proven reserves of natural gas amounted to 75 trillion cubic feet or 2.1 trillion cubic meters--21 percent of total hydrocarbon reserves. The reserves/production figure was estimated as 51 years; if the Chicontepec Basin reserves are excluded, this figure drops to 33 years. Attention should be drawn to the fact that the oil reserves/production figure is slightly higher, averaging 57 years.

Recent experience has shown Mexico's natural gas market system to be more flexible than was originally envisaged. On the demand side, the domestic market has managed to absorb all available gas. During the last five years, PEMEX's own gas consumption has grown at an average annual rate of 20 percent, while the growth rate of total sales to industry has averaged 10 percent, notwithstanding supply restrictions in 1982. Moreover, a substantial increase in the use of natural gas for electricity generation is plausible. This potential demand could rapidly become effective, as most of the larger power stations are equipped with dual burners capable of using heavy fuel oil or natural gas. It is fair to conclude that at present domestic prices, demand far exceeds available supplies.

On the supply size, the system's flexibility stems, first, from the discretionary margin allowed by nonassociated gas fields in determining output levels. Second, it is also possible to vary gas production levels associated with certain oil output levels: disparities exist in the gas/oil ratios of onshore fields, as well as between these and the offshore areas in the Bay of Campeche. Thus, variegation in the geographical sites of crude production can significantly affect the total volume of associated gas that is produced. One example is sufficient to illustrate this point. The Agave field in the Reforma area yields 50 thousand barrels per day (b/d) of light crude oil and 450 million cf/d of natural gas, that is, a gas/oil ratio of 9,000 cubic feet of gas per barrel of oil. In contrast, the average gas/oil ratio in the Cantarell field off Campeche is twenty times smaller.

Another important source of flexibility is to be found in the size and extent of the pipeline system that links production and processing facilities with the main consuming areas of the country and with the U.S. border. Presently, the gas transport system is integrated by more than 7,004 miles (11,270 kilometers) of pipeline, serving all the large industrial cities and the major industrial ports. The flexibility inherent in this system has elicited much controversy in the last few years: opinions have altered drastically--both domestically and abroad--with regard to the actual volume of surplus gas available for export and the role exports should play in terms of Mexico's natural gas system. Initially, massive exports were seen as the only alternative to the flaring of natural gas; more recently, the view has prevailed that gas exports should play only a marginal role and that priority should be given to its domestic use. And in fact, if the present pattern and rate of growth of domestic demand continue, it will not be feasible to increase exports during 1984.

The flaring of natural gas in Mexico is the result of inadequate planning and a lack of coordination of investment programs in crude oil production facilities and in gas-gathering, processing, and transport systems. Over the last five years the expansion of these systems has been particularly unbalanced, and serious bottlenecks have appeared. The construction of natural gas infrastructure has lagged behind oil production, reflecting the higher priority accorded the rapid growth of crude exports as well as supplier disinterest in making domestic sales of natural gas, due in part to low domestic prices, which in some areas were even lower than the cost of transporting the gas. Coordinating oil and gas programs has been the more difficult, given the fast pace at which offshore fields in Campeche were developed--where oil was first produced in mid-1979 and current output flows at a rate of 1.6 million b/d.

Detailed statistical analyses confirm that gas flaring has not been a consequence of inadequate domestic demand. Medium- and long-term projections show that domestic demand can absorb all the gas produced under a wide range of alternative assumptions. These studies categorically conclude that the portrayal of Mexico's options as "to export gas or to flare it" continues to be misleading. Accurate characterizations of policy options must consider several variables: increases in domestic consumption and the possibility of shutting in significant quantities of gas, as well as additional exports.

The nature of these options gives Mexico a solid negotiating position with respect to exports. The existence of a wide variety of alternative uses for Mexican natural gas increases the value of this resource. Investment decisions in energy-intensive activities and processes must take into account the opportunity cost of gas. Export projects and the pricing of exports should give due consideration to alternative uses of gas within the country. The implications of different intertemporal consumption patterns must be explored. Under these conditions policy design and decision making become more complex. This is why Mexico's large and diversified energy resource endowment poses particularly interesting questions.

GAS EXPORTS

In world terms, Mexico is an important natural gas producer and only a minor participant in its international trade. The size and rapid growth of its domestic market have limited the amount available for export. However, Mexico's export potential is widely recognized due to its large resource base, its ample possibilities for domestic interfuel substitution, its underutilized pipeline capacity to the north of the country, and its contiguity to the largest natural gas market in the world (the United States).

Five years ago the prospect of Mexico's becoming a large-scale exporter seemed imminent as PEMEX negotiated a 2 billion cf/d (20.7 billion) export contract. These negotiations were particularly complex and entailed difficult noncommercial aspects. They began in early 1977 and concluded in October of 1979 with the signing of a contract for only 300 million cf/d (29 million cm). Negotiations between PEMEX and Border Gas, the U.S. consortium, gave way to government talks, and the question of natural gas trade became a key issue in U.S.-Mexican relations. Within both countries an intense debate took place with respect to Mexican gas exports. In the United States, these negotiations coincided with the discussion, adoption, and initial implementation of the Natural Gas Policy Act, along with other legislation that directly affected natural gas markets. In Mexico, the gas export question instigated a wide-ranging and heated debate on such issues as the role of oil and gas exports in long-term development and in short-term economic management, the oil industry's expansion strategy, and the nature of bilateral relations between the two countries, as well as specific technical and economic questions regarding the construction of the pipeline that would deliver gas to the U.S. border.[1]

During 1981 Mexico exported 288 million cf/d (27 million cm) of natural gas, earning $53 million. The current export price, like the Canadian, is $4.94 per million Btu. In the short run, it is not possible to increase natural gas exports. With additional compressor capacity onstream by the fourth quarter of 1982, the trunkline to northern Mexico can transport a greater volume of gas. But there is a second, longer-term constraint on natural gas exports: gas-processing facilities in the southern producing areas are operating at full capacity and their expansion has not been feasible before this year (1983), when two new 500 million cf/d (48 million cm) cryogenic plants will be operational. Until that date, the only way to increase the exportable gas surplus is by restricting domestic consumption via measures to promote natural gas substitution. Substitution programs will have to concentrate initially on the oil industry itself and on other large public sector consumers with dual burner facilities.

Eventually, it will be necessary to extend these efforts to the rest of the industry. This presupposes a drastic change in the relative prices of natural gas and heavy fuel oil. Unfortunately, it is difficult to forecast the rate at which interfuel substitution will take place.

The long-term expansion of Mexican natural gas exports will require adequate incentives. Given alternative domestic uses of natural gas, a rapidly expanding domestic energy market, and the possibility of satisfying foreign-exchange requirements through oil exports, the warranted price of Mexican gas might not be compatible with pricing principles that relate this hydrocarbon to residual fuel oil. From a Mexican perspective the main reasons for this discrepancy are:

1. Within the country natural gas directly substitutes not only for fuel oil but also for diesel, LPG (liquid petroleum gas), and indirectly, other fuels.
2. Natural gas also substitutes crude for oil. By upgrading refineries, overall domestic crude requirements are reduced. On a Btu basis, the greater the price gap between crude oil and gas, the larger the incentive to invest in refinery flexibility.
3. At a given price, large industrial consumers are not indifferent between gas and residual fuel. Greater maintenance, storage, and inventory costs arise when fuel oil is burned. Externalities must also be considered.
4. Gas supply arrangements are necessarily more rigid than those relating to oil. They are also more vulnerable insofar as Mexican gas exports supply only one highly regulated market (the United States).

PETROCHEMICALS

PEMEX is the largest natural gas consumer is Mexico. The national oil company uses this hydrocarbon as a fuel in its fields, pipeline systems, and refineries; in power generation; and, increasingly, as a raw material in basic petrochemical production. It is interesting to note that gas consumption by PEMEX grew at an average annual rate of 20 percent during the last five years, whereas heavy oil use increased by only 1 percent per year. Recent estimates indicate that basic petrochemical production accounts for 9 percent of total hydrocarbon use in Mexico. This year (1983) 12 million tons of 42 basic petrochemicals will be produced in 97 plants. This output satisfies 85 percent of total domestic requirements. Although the overall degree of self-sufficiency will increase over the next few years, this process will become more selective, and specific product deficits will be met through processing and swapping arrangements.

Production of ammonia and methanol is the most intensive natural gas-using activity within PEMEX. In 1981 ammonia output reached 2.2 million tons, 35 percent of which was exported. Production and exports should increase significantly since two 445,000-ton plants came onstream in 1982. It is well known that at current prices for ammonia, the netback on the gas used in production for export is extremely low. Thus it is likely that construction of two additional 445,000-ton plants, now in the engineering stage, is linked instead to efforts to increase domestic urea production capacity and is consistent with overall policy objectives: to reach self-sufficiency in fertilizer products, to gradually reduce intermediate product exports, and to develop export capacity in high-quality fertilizers.

The level of methanol output is much more modest. In 1982, 180,000 tons were produced and exports represented 17 percent of this total. Although engineering work has been done on two 825,000-ton plants, actual construction has been postponed. A gasoline/methanol mix for automobile use in high altitudes is under careful study; this mix could improve combustion and reduce pollution in the Mexico City metropolitan area. Additional capacity for methanol production can only be justified by massive transport use. As in the case of ammonia, the low netback on the natural gas used in methanol exports does not justify further investment in this area.

By law, only PEMEX can produce and sell all first-generation petrochemicals, as well as an important number of second-generation products. Except for fertilizer production, which is also exclusively a public sector activity, the remainder of secondary and tertiary petrochemical production transpires in the private sector, where joint ventures prevail. Domestic production of secondary petrochemicals satisfies 80 percent of domestic demand, and current imports cover only a small proportion of total import requirements. Current expansion programs should increase self-sufficiency to about 90 percent by 1985.

The growth and diversification of the Mexican petrochemical industry will continue during the 1980s. Its expansion is firmly based on abundant raw materials, an industrial infrastructure capable of handling large-scale projects, an increasing capacity for selecting and adapting complex technologies, and good engineering capabilities. These resources should allow the industry to cope with the rapid expansion of domestic demand. It is important to emphasize that Mexico is still in the high growth phase of the petrochemical product cycle. Parallel to efforts in the domestic market, the petrochemical industry must also expand exports in order to pay for a larger proportion of its own intermediate product imports.

Special mention must be made of the fertilizer industry. Its resource base is unique. The country is endowed with natural gas for ammonia production as well as large-scale sulfur resources in southern Mexico and large phosphoric rock deposits and feasible potassium recovery projects in Baja California. At present, the domestic fertilizer market absorbs 4.5 million tons of fertilizer per year, 85 percent of which is produced locally. Mexico is a country of more than 70 million people, and by the end of this century its population will have surpassed 110 million. Today, it is self-sufficient in basic foodstuffs and has traditionally exported agricultural products. If this situation is to continue, fertilizer production must increase at a very rapid pace. In addition, the production of an export surplus in fertilizer is appropriate: such exports could be an important source of foreign exchange and, more basically, a means by which energy may add value to other natural resources. An export promotion scheme will require serious planning and coordination efforts within the public sector, as all the input and final product industries involved are state-owned.

OTHER INDUSTRIAL CONSUMERS

Other large-scale consumers of natural gas in Mexico are the electricity, steel, cement, gas, paper and pulp, and mining sectors. In electricity generation, natural gas is mainly utilized in gas turbines. Its use in boilers lends flexibility to gas-load management and is basically restricted to smoothing out weekly and seasonal load variations. On short notice, the electricity sector could drastically increase its consumption of natural gas.

In Latin America, Mexico's steel industry is second only to that of Brazil. Last year its output reached 7.6 million tons. This industry uses large quantities of gas, both as a fuel and raw material. Of total output, 24 percent was obtained from DRI (directly reduced iron) plants; Hylsa, the Mexican firm that developed the direct reduction process that bears its name, is the largest single private consumer of natural gas. Technological choice in this industry has important implications in terms of energy efficiency and with respect to the primary and secondary energy mix. The relative role that DRI and other processes should play in the expansion of the steel industry poses particularly interesting and challenging problems for project appraisal and sectoral planning.

In recent years the cement, glass, and paper and pulp industries have developed rapidly in response to domestic demand and have generated a modest level of both exports and imports. In 1981 these industries' consumption of natural gas was 80 million, 70 million, and 50 million cf/d (7.7 million, 6.8 million, and 4.8 million cm), respectively. These branches also use large quantities of liquid fuels and electricity.

PRIORITIES IN GAS DEVELOPMENT

The highest priority has been given to the elimination of natural gas flaring in the Bay of Campeche. Last year total gas flaring represented 21 percent of gross associated gas production. In the onshore fields this figure was less than 5 percent. However, all gas produced in Campeche was flared. Now a gas-gathering system is in place; a 36-inch pipeline to onshore processing facilities is operational. Gas started to flow in December 1982 and the portion processed is now 40 percent of gross output. In addition, 100 million cf/d compressor modules are coming onstream at a rapid pace. Flaring from the Cantarell field will end during the third quarter of 1983 and in the fourth quarter in the other offshore fields under production.

High priority is assigned as well to balancing the natural gas system and to eliminating bottlenecks. This will increase the productivity of recent investment and provide a modest increase in net output. It will also prepare the system for projected increases in gas availability this year.

There is great potential for natural gas conservation, particularly within the oil industry. The very low price that is imputed to gas in intrafirm accounts explains the highly inefficient use of this fuel. This is similarly the case in the rest of the industry: low domestic prices have contributed to waste. It is possible to achieve significant gas savings through simple substitution measures and better housekeeping.

A better allocation of available natural gas must be pursued. Large-size boiler use should be gradually restricted, and greater attention must be given to developing and serving premium markets. Low domestic prices increase the risk of stimulating production processes and activities that are profitable from a private perspective but do not necessarily generate value added for the economy as a whole.

In order to futher these policy objectives a more realistic and active price policy will have to be implemented. Recent increases in domestic prices of fuel oil and natural gas are steps in the right direction. On June 1, 1983, the price of gas increased from $0.34 per million Btu to $0.54 and will be automatically adjusted at a monthly rate of 5 percent. The price of fuel oil will increase at the same rate from its present level of $3.46 per barrel, including transport. In Btu terms the price of gas is only 5 percent higher than that of heavy fuel oil. This differential will have to be increased gradually so that surplus fuel oil will replace natural gas in low-priority markets.

NOTES

1. The history of these negotiations has been documented mostly by U.S. authors, and the treatment given to the interaction between domestic and export markets has been inadequate and frequently in error. This has proved to be a major limitation in the analysis of the negotiating process and its outcome.

5
Coal in Mexico

Miguel Castaneda
Roberto Iza

From 1921 to 1940, small coal companies proliferated in Mexico, with a few larger ones starting production. The cumulative coal produced was 32 million tons, most of which was coking coal from the state of Coahuila.

Coal became increasingly more important after 1950, and this trend has continued as a result of the development of the iron and steel industry (the main consumer of this raw material) and the mining and metallurgy industries. (See Table 5.1 for coal and coke production and importation figures.) And, beginning in 1960, Mexico began using coal to generate electricity. The Federal Commission of Electricity was in charge of systematically exploring the coal basin of Fuentes-Rio Escondido in the state of Coahuila; it discovered that there were sufficient reserves to supply the thermal-electric plant of Nava, Coahuila, which operated until 1978 with an installed capacity of 37.5 megawatts (MW).

This activity enabled the Federal Commission of Electricity to establish its own exploration department, which was given the name "Northeast Coal Studies" and was part of the National Coal Program. The department continued exploring the Fuentes-Rio Escondido basin and carrying out investigations in the Tertiary deposits in the region of Colombia-Nuevo Laredo as well as in other states in Mexico.

COAL PROVINCES AND EVIDENCE OF COAL IN MEXICO

Coal deposits are found throughout Mexico, but economically important reserves are located in only three regions: (1) the northeast, where most of the known reserves are distributed in the Cretaceous basins of Fuentes-Rio Escondido and Sabinas in the state of Coahuila and in the Tertiary basin of Colombia-Nuevo Laredo in the states of Nuevo Leon and Tamaulipas; (2) the northwest (Sonora), in the Cretaceous basin of Cabullona in the northern part of the state of Sonora and in the basin containing the

Table 5.1
Production and Importation of Coal and Coal By-Products (tons)

	1970	1971	1972	1973	1974	1975	1976	1977	1978	1979	1980
Coal Production											
Noncoking coal	121,000	85,000	110,000	118,000	181,255	176,839	156,152	247,863	154,806	62,000	330,830
Coking coal	2,838,024	3,427,595	3,503,929	4,145,137	4,983,784	5,013,709	5,493,476	6,362,360	6,600,750	7,294,696	6,792,000
Others					700	2,900					
Total	2,959,024	3,512,595	3,613,929	4,263,137	5,165,739	5,193,448	5,649,628	6,610,223	6,755,556	7,356,696	7,122,830
Coke Production											
Metallurgical coke					2,034,011	2,057,703	2,151,523	2,814,660	2,807,503	2,589,338	
Imperial coke					16,885	12,480	20,775	12,069	11,195	13,444	
Fine coke					19,711	17,821	15,559	65,051	87,198	64,588	
Total	1,299,553	1,608,344	1,755,519	1,934,471	2,070,607	2,088,004	2,187,857	2,891,780	2,905,923	2,667,370	2,409,228
Coal Imports											
Washed coal	151,018	262,173	379,829	229,963	365,459	447,030	88,460	624,991	759,801	733,540	823,000
Lignite and agglomerates	2,096		2,391	7,340	2,613	3,315	3,000	4,195	5,290	7,539	
Peat	140		313	838	433	245	91	550	1,944	403	
Retorting coal	614		3	226	784	3	273	245	455	202	
Activated coal	820				1,437	120	200	1,356	6,213	313	
Activated coal (granular)						394	1,608	4,203	30,888	1,611	
Total	154,688	163,359*	388,604*	238,367	370,726	451,107	93,632	635,540	804,591	743,608	
Coke Imports											
Metallurgical coke	340,322	68,156	132,467	140,232	171,444	105,835	96,045	41,370	249,238	126,781	110,000
Tar coke			1,474	9,793	15,008	7,175	212	587	11,661	14,937	
Petroleum coke					133,472	166,682	97,652	177,267	321,471	188,103	
Others											
Total	460,322*	249,235*	435,648*	475,308*	319,924	279,692	193,909	219,224	582,370	329,821	

*Data incomplete

Source: Prepared by the authors for the Mexican Energy Commission based on primary data, 1981.

Triassic-Jurassic Barranca formation, which extends from San Marcial to Alamos; and (3) the south, in the Tlaxiaco, Niltepec, and Tezoatlan basins, all Jurassic and located in the state of Oaxaca. Coal occurrences in the just-mentioned states and elsewhere have been occasionally explored, but there has been little in-depth study. Both governmental as well as private groups, primarily the Mineral Resource Council, have undertaken this exploration, but to date the geologic characteristics have not been defined. The most important areas with coal occurrences are listed below.

Southern Baja California: Graphite occurs in the area around San Antonio El Triunfo.

Coahuila: In addition to the three areas already mentioned, there is evidence of coal in Cuatro Cienegas and Los Alamos, and of peat in Parras.

Chiapas: Bituminous coal occurs in Palenque and Tonala.

Chihuahua: There are many important occurrences of sub-bituminous coal in the Ojinaga basin, which, because of its geologic similarity to the basins in Coahuila, is currently being explored by the Federal Commission of Electricity. Other areas include San Pedro Corralitos and Caleta with shows of anthracite and Ciudad Juarez with occurrences of lignite.

Colima: Armeria lignite.

Durango: Areas with bituminous coal have been reported around Nazas, anthracite near Cuencame, and unclassified coal near Santiago Papasquiaro.

Guerrero: Some areas with coal and lignite around Chilpancingo.

Hidalgo: There is some evidence of lignite and/or peat in Tehuichila, Zacualtipan, and San Miguel Ocaxichitlan and other areas with coal near Tulancingo, Ixtacamaxtitlan, and Jacala.

Jalisco: Lignite in Etzatlan, peat in Sayula, and coal in Concepcion de Buenos Aires.

Mexico: Occurrences of coal in Chalco and Valle de Bravo.

Michoacan: Bituminous coal, anthracite, and lignite have been reported around the town of Huetamo.

Nayarit: Peat occurs near Tepic.

Nuevo Leon: Besides the coal in the Tertiary basin of Colombia-Nuevo Laredo, there is evidence of lignite and bituminous coal in the southern part of the state near Galeana and Dr. Arroyo.

Oaxaca: In addition to the coal in the Jurassic basins already mentioned, there is evidence of bituminous coal in the eastern part of the state near Niltepec.

Puebla: Presence of bituminous coal in Ixtacamaxtitlan, San Martin Texmelucan, Acatlan, Tecomatlan, and Zautla.

San Luis Potosi: There is some lignite in Cretaceous sediments near Xilitla, Coaxcatlan, and Temexcalco and shows of sub-bituminous coal in Tertiary rocks near Tamazunchale that have no apparent interest.

Sonora: In addition to the coal found in the already mentioned basins, there are several mines and evidence of graphite near Alamos-San Bernardo.

Tlaxcala: Coal is known to exist near Huilapan, Huexoyucan, and Tenetzontla.

Veracruz: There is evidence of bituminous coal in Cretaceous sediments near Panuco, Tanscasneque, and Tempoal; there are occurrences of sub-bituminous coal in Tertiary sediments near Chicontepec, and coal is present in Yahualica, Ayuquila, Tlacoalulan, and Chinameca.

RESERVES AND RESOURCES: DEFINITIONS

There are many differences of opinion concerning the subject of coal reserves and resources in Mexico due to the diverse criteria used to evaluate and define them. This lack of agreement has complicated the quantitative interpretation as well as the qualitative definition of these reserves and resources. Evaluation criteria within the iron and steel industry differ from one company to the next and even within the various governmental offices that explore for coal. These criteria will not be discussed in this chapter, as the subject is much too broad.

This problem does not exist only in Mexico; other countries have still not made a clear distinction between exactly what constitutes a resource. The U.S. Geological Survey defines a resource as "a concentration of naturally occurring solid, liquid, or gaseous material, in or on the earth's crust, that is in such form that economic extraction is currently or potentially feasible." Resources can be divided into identified and undiscovered, based on the amount of available geologic knowledge. Identified resources include reserves, which are defined as "that part of an identified resource that can be economically exploited at the time of its classification." For the purposes of this chapter, the following terms and definitions will be used.

Proven Reserve: The amount of coal that is calculated to exist based on knowledge gainde from direct development work and/or drilling of boreholes that are spaced in a manner such that the geologic characteristics, size, form, and composition of the area under study are reliably established with a certainty within a range of plus or minus 20 percent.

Probable Reserve: The amount of coal that may exist as defined by extension and correlation controls in a studied area based on evidence from field studies and/or drilling of boreholes that are spaced such that the coal cannot be placed among proven reserves.

Possible Reserve: The amount of coal that has been

estimated to exist based on stratigraphic and structural controls, on indirect (geophysical) interpretations, on scattered evidence, or on results obtained from isolated drilling, sampling, and other exploratory work. The accuracy of the estimates is less than that for probable reserves.

Additional Resource: Coal that is assumed or supposed to exist based on preliminary studies, miscellaneous information, proper geologic environment for deposition, the presence of outcroppings, on stratigraphic correlation with other regions, etc.

Recoverable or Exploitable Reserve: Coal that can be extracted from the surface and used as a raw material, under the technical and economic conditions that exist at the time it is evaluated, based on pre-feasibility and detailed studies, on regional experience, etc.

Coal Potential: The total estimated quantity of coal described in the above definitions.

It must be noted that the above definitions may differ in concept and interpretation from those used by others.

Coal has been classified according to various systems, the most important of which has been established by the A.S.T.M. (American Society Testing of Materials). The A.S.T.M. system is based on the ratio between fixed carbon and volatile matter in an agglomerated state. For high-rank coal, it additionally takes into account the content of fixed carbon and volatile matter over a dry, ash-free base; for low-rank coal, it considers potential Btu (British thermal unit) content over a wet, ash-free base. The classifications are shown in Table 5.2.

Table 5.2
The A.S.T.M. System of Coal Classification

Type of Coal	Percent of Fixed Carbon	Percent of Volatile Matter
Anthracite		
Meta-anthracite	98-100	0-2
Anthracite	92-98	2-8
Semi-anthracite	86-92	8-14
Bituminous		
Low-volatile matter	78-86	14-22
Medium-volatile matter	69-78	22-31
High-volatile matter	69	31
Lignite	50-69	40-50

Coal in the known coal-bearing regions in Mexico has been classified as follows. (1) The Sabinas, Saltillito, Las Esperanzas, and San Patricio basins in the state of Coahuila contain medium- to low-volatile bituminous coal. Most of this coal has good physical agglomeration characteristics, allowing it to be converted to coke. (2) The region of Fuentes-Rio Escondido in the state of Coahuila possesses high-volatile, high-flaming bituminous coal. In general, coal from this region cannot be converted to coke due to its physical and chemical properties. (3) The region of Teozotlan-Mixtepec and Consuelo in Oaxaca contains anthracite, semi-anthracite, and bituminous coal. (4) The region of Santa Clara and San Marcial in Sonora contains anthracite and meta-anthracite coal. The coal from areas 3 and 4 cannot be converted to coke. In some areas, natural coke exists.

For the purposes of this chapter, coal will be categorized into two types: that which can and that which cannot be converted into coke, based on its characteristics, properties of agglomeration, and provenance. The first type is used as coke for the steel and metallurgical industries and the second is used to generate electrical power.

RESERVES AND RESOURCES: ESTIMATES

State of Coahuila

At the present time, the coal deposits in Coahuila are considered the most important, based on completed studies. There are two coal fields in this state: Sabinas, which extends as far as Monclova and is divided into several sub-basins, and the Fuentes-Rio Escondido basin, which probably extends from Piedras Negras to San Ignacio in the State of Tamaulipas.

In the Sabinas field, the coal is mostly coking coal, and therefore is reserved to meet the needs of the growing iron and steel industry of the north. In the second area, the coal is high-flaming bituminous, which apparently cannot be converted to coke and is devoted to the generation of electrical power.

According to the Ministry of National Wealth and Industrial Development (Secretaria de Patrimonio y Fomento Industrial), the in situ coking coal reserves in the Sabinas field were conservatively estimated at 1.5 billion tons as of the end of 1980. However, the probable reserves plus proven reserves estimate is the object of speculation, with estimates ranging between 800 million and 1.4 billion tons. If the possible reserves in the Sabinas field are verified, there will be between 2.3 and 2.9 billion tons of in situ coking coal reserves, which will ensure that the growing needs of the iron and steel industry will be met at least through 2010. Even with the currently proven reserves, it is estimated that the iron and steel industry's needs will be met until the year 2000; hence, they have some time to evaluate the probable reserves through exploration programs with the goal of increasing the reserves at a rate of at least 75 million tons per year.

As for the Fuentes-Rio Escondido field, exploration and studies carried out by various companies and governmental institutions revealed proven and probable in situ reserves as of the end of 1980 to be as listed in Table 5.3.

Table 5.3
Coal Reserves in Coahuila, the Fuentes-Rio Escondido Field (millions of tons)

	Rank A	Rank B	Total
Proven Reserves			
1960-1978	174	19	193
1978-1980	140	130	170
Probable Reserves	40	123	163
Total	354	272	626

The figures were modified at the end of 1981, as a result of studies and exploration carried out by the Federal Commission of Electricity that year. The commission estimated proven rank A and B reserves to be 576 million tons; probable rank A and B reserves, 140 million tons; and possible rank A and B reserves, 185 million tons--for a total reserve of 901 million tons. (Rank A reserves are those with a seam thickness of more than 1.30 meters, and rank B are those with a thickness between 0.8 and 1.30 meters.) In addition, these same studies have permitted estimates of additional resources in the province of around 350 million tons in situ.

State of Tamaulipas

Around the city of Nuevo Laredo, drilling carried out in the Colombia-Nuevo Laredo basin has allowed estimates of proven reserves at 44 million tons, probable reserves at 55 million tons, and possible reserves at 100 million tons. The coal in this area has about 30 percent more Btu (British thermal units) content than the coal of the Fuentes-Rio Escondido basin. Because of the larger size of the basin under study as well as the favorable geologic conditions, additional resources are estimated at 500 millions tons in situ.

State of Oaxaca

Exploration carried out by the National Coal Program and studies developed by the National Resource Council have enabled the exploitable reserves in El Consuelo basins in Tezoatlan, Oaxaca, to be initially evaluated. Exploration has not yet been completed, yet reserves are estimated at 100 million tons, according to a National Resource Council report.

The Federal Commission of Electricity has provided the figures shown in Table 5.4 for sub-bituminous coal.

Table 5.4
Sub-Bituminous Coal in Oaxaca, El Consuelo Basins (millions of tons)

	Proven	Probable	Possible	Total
Tezoatlan	--	30	30	60
Tlaxiaco	17	--	--	17
Total	17	30	30	77

Drilling by the Mineral Resource Council around Tlaxiaco-Tezoatlan has blocked out 100 million tons with speculations of 200 million tons; however, it is expected that the potential is even greater. Furthermore, in a National Resource Council report of June 1980 concerning the results of exploration carried out by the National Coal Exploration Plan, the blocked-out reserves are: San Juan Viejo area, 1.34 million tons; Plaza de Lobos area, 7.62 million tons; Plancha El Consuelo area, 2.36 million tons; and Numi area, 20.55 million tons.

A great deal of information is available on the reserves in Oaxaca, but the data are uneven. There are discrepancies in the figures and in the geographic location, possibly due to the little exploration that has been carried out and to the fact that the work has been done by various companies and governmental organizations. The discrepancies may also be due to the lack of systematic exploration and to the questionable nature of the sources of information. In light of these facts, the Federal Commission of Electricity decided to adopt the following figures: proven reserves, 17 million tons; probable reserves, 30 million tons; possible reserves, 30 million tons; and additional resources, 200 million tons. Table 5.5 presents further information on reserve estimates since 1970 for all of Mexico.

Table 5.5
All Varieties of Coal, Washed Coal, and Coke, 1970-1980 (tons)

	All Varieties	Washed Coal	Coke
1970	2,959,024	1,345,130	1,299,553
1971	3,512,595	1,547,315	1,588,688
1972	3,613,929	1,587,752	1,755,519
1973	4,263,137	1,846,814	1,934,471
1974	5,165,739	2,203,884	2,070,697
1975	5,193,449	2,190,575	2,088,004
1976	5,649,623	2,449,384	2,187,857
1977	6,610,223	2,915,676	2,891,780
1978	6,755,556	3,084,564	2,905,923
1979	7,356,696	3,124,938	2,667,370
1980	7,122,830	2,681,000	2,409,228

Source: Prepared by the authors for the Mexican Energy Commission based on primary data, 1981.

State of Sonora

A similar situation occurs in the reserve estimates for the state of Sonora. The figures for anthracite coal reserves provided by the federal commission are given in Table 5.6, and the Mineral Resource Council estimate of

Table 5.6
Anthracite Coal in Sonora, Estimated by the Federal Commission (millions of tons)

	Proven	Probable	Possible	Total
San Marcial	4	9	18	31
Santa Clara	2	--	71	73
Total	6	9	89	104

coal reserves is given in Table 5.7. As can be seen, there is a discrepancy in the quantity of reserves, categories, and regions; for that reason and for the purposes of this chapter, the following figures on reserves and resources will be used for the areas of San Marcial, Santa Clara, and San Enrique: proven reserves, 6 million tons; probable reserves, 9 million tons; possible reserves, 160 million tons; and additional resources,

100 million tons.

Table 5.7
Coal in Sonora, Estimated by the Mineral Resources Council (millions of tons)

	Proven	Probable	Possible	Total
San Marcial	--	--	--	--
Santa Clara	0.7	--	17.5	18.2
San Enrique	2.0	--	71.0	73.0
Total	2.7	--	88.5	91.2

State of Chihuahua

The Ojinaga coal basin has an area of 3,000 square kilometers, in which isolated sites have been explored leading to an estimate of 40 million possible tons of in situ sub-bituminous coal and 400 million tons of additional resources. To date, the Federal Commission of Electricity has been working on regional geologic explorations in the areas of Ojinaga-San Carlos and San Pedro-Corralitos. It is said that further exploration programs will enable the tonnages to be verified and even increased (adding to the attractiveness of these areas), even though organizations such as the Mineral Resource Council have given statements to the contrary and downplayed these areas in Chihuahua as a result of studies and exploration they have carried out.

SUMMARY

To summarize the figures for estimated coal reserves and resources, as of June 1982, the nation's noncoking coal that can be used to generate electricity stands at proven reserves, 643 million tons; probable reserves, 244 million tons; possible reserves, 515 million tons; and additional resources, 1,750 million tons--for a total of 3,152 million tons. A breakdown by location is given in Table 5.8. According to a study made by the Institute of Steel Research and the Institute of Electrical Power Research and sponsored by the Energy Resources Commission, if the iron and steel industry continued to wash all varieties of coal to obtain a product yielding 15 to 18 percent ash, and mixtures yielding as much as 45 percent ash were obtained from the washing plants, 1,116,864 tons of mixed coal could be obtained with a Btu content of 4,500 kilocalories per kilogram, using the 1979 production of coking coal. This production of mixed coal could feed

Table 5.8
Reserves and Resources of Noncoking Coal, as of June 1982 (millions of tons, in situ)

State and Location	Reserves			Resources	Total
	Proven	Probable	Possible		
Coahuila					
Fuentes-Rio Escondido	576	140	185	350	1,251
Tamaulipas					
Colombia-Nuevo Laredo	44	65	100	300	509
Sonora					
San Marcial	4	9	18	100	131
Santa Clara	2	--	71	--	73
San Enrique	--	--	71	--	71
Cabullona	--	--	--	400	400
Chihuahua					
Ojinaga-San Carlos	--	--	40	250	290
San Pedro-Corralitos	--	--	--	150	150
Oaxaca					
Tezoatlan and Tlaxiaco	17	30	30	200	277
Total	643	244	515	1,750	3,152

a coal-electric plant with an installed capacity of 300 MW, consuming 2,960 kilocalories per kilowatt hour generated and working with a load factor of 70 percent.

With this order of magnitude in mind, if it were decided in the future to produce mixtures, these would supply the following accumulated on-line coal-electric plant capacity for the given years: 730 MW for 1985, 1,200 MW for 1990, 1,800 MW for 1995, and 2,650 MW for 2000. Based on studies carried out by the Energy Resources Commission in 1976, there are approximately 225 million tons of proven reserves in seams between 0.7 and 1.10 meters thick located in mining concessions owned by steel companies and in areas relinquished by them that are now owned by the Mining Development Commission. These reserves, using actual economic criteria from the energy point of view, could meet the demand of a 1,400 MW coal-electric plant.

Thus, the reserves of coal in Mexico offer a viable means of expanding the nation's energy resources base. Although the coal is there, its development will be linked to the economics of its exploitation as related to the cost of other energies and especially Mexico's other hydrocarbons--crude oil and natural gas.

6
Research and Development in Geothermal Energy

Sergio Mercado
Pablo Mulas

Geothermal projects to generate electricity, like hydroelectric or thermal-electric projects, are the responsibility of the Mexican Federal Commission of Electricity (CFE). The Mexican Electrical Power Research Institute (IIE) carries out research and development projects to support the CFE in the construction and operation of geothermal-electric plants.

Development of geothermal energy in Mexico is centered primarily in two large geothermal regions, the Valley of Mexicali and the Neo-volcanic Axis. The majority of the 400 hydrothermally altered sites that have been classified to date have been found in these regions.

Greater geothermal development has occurred in the Valley of Mexicali, located in northwestern Mexico. In 1973, two power plant units, each generating 37.5 MW (megawatts), began operation using separated steam at a pressure of 5.3 kg/cm^2 (kilograms per square centimeter) produced from wells. In 1979, two similar units came on line, increasing installed capacity to 150 MW.

The wells that feed the units of the Cerro Prieto I plant produce a steam-water mixture. Each well has a separator operating at 7 kg/cm^2. The steam goes to the generator and the brine to an evaporation lagoon, thereby wasting a vast amount of energy. After analyzing the situation, the IIE brought to the CFE's attention the feasibility of generating an additional 30 MW by means of flash evaporation of the hot brine at pressures of 3.5 and 1.5 kg/cm^2 using a double pressure-stage turbine. This turbine became operational in 1981.

There are currently two other plants under construction: Cerro Prieto II and Cerro Prieto III. These plants will each have two 110 MW units, giving the Cerro Prieto installation an installed capacity of 620 MW by 1985.

Near Cerro Prieto in the Valley of Mexicali, deep exploration is being conducted. Medium and high temperature gradients have been detected in wells drilled at Riito, Tulechek, and Aeropuerto where the probability of finding economically exploitable reserves is good. The potential capacity in the Valley of Mexicali has been estimated at around 1,500 MW.

The other geothermal region, the Neo-volcanic Axis, is located in the central part of the country. The region consists of a strip several kilometers wide and 900 km long, with more than 3,000 volcanic features and a great number of hydrothermal shows. Surface exploration and deep drilling are currently being carried out at fifteen sites, with efforts being concentrated at Los Azufres in the state of Michoacan, La Primavera in Jalisco, and Los Humeros in Pueblo.

Thirty wells have been drilled at Los Azufres. Most of them are excellent producers with sufficient steam for an installed capacity of 90 MW. Preliminary studies of the reservoir indicate a potential capacity of 300 MW. The first unit at Los Azufres will have a capacity of 55 MW and will go on line in 1986. There are currently five 5 MW units installed at a wellhead. Two of these operate with dry steam and the other three with wet stream, requiring the residual brine to be reinjected due to a high boron content.

There are four exploratory wells at the La Primavera field, located a few kilometers from Guadalajara. All have a high bottom temperature and average wet steam production.

Four deep exploratory wells have been drilled at the Los Humeros field, with excellent results. Bottom temperatures are over 300° C, with separated steam wells producing up to 70 tons/hour and one dry steam well.

The CFE plans to attain an installed capacity of at least 4,000 MW by the year 2000, a goal considered entirely feasible based on the results obtained from the exploration efforts already detailed. To assist the CFE with that project, the Geothermal Program was established by IIE in 1977. This program was structured to encourage direct consultation among personnel from the CFE, universities, and the IIE. Four of the five divisions of the institute participate in the program: Energy Sources, Engineering Studies, Equipment and Training, and Communications. Seventy researchers and twenty technicians are currently working on a full-time basis.

The objective was to set priorities for solving problems that had a practical bearing on the design and operation of the power plants. Because the IIE had been only recently created, it was necessary to develop a personnel as well as a laboratory infrastructure. It was decided that the institute would not duplicate the activities of existing groups with pertinent expertise, but would lend its support through contracts and subsidies. The program can be surveyed by grouping its activities in three categories: exploration, field development, and exploitation, including the generation of electrical power.

EXPLORATION

Because geophysical research groups were already in existence in Mexico, the institute opted to support and and assist them. With the financial backing of the commission and the United Nations Development Program (UNDP), three projects were conceived with research groups from the Ensenada Center of Scientific Investigation and Higher Education (CICESE) and from the Institute of Geophysics and Research in Applied Mathematics and Systems of the University of Mexico. The former group developed the methodology and obtained information to model the geologic faults in the Valley of Mexicali, using the results of observations made during microseismic events. These studies have been continued at the Cerro Prieto field, and some observations have been made around the Los Azufres and La Primavera fields. With commission and UNDP backing, the same group of geophysicists from CICESE has developed the means to evaluate the usefulness of the magnetotelluric method in geothermal exploration. Their first field study has been completed in the area of Culiacan, Sinaloa, and their next observations will be made around the Los Azufres and Cuitzeo fields. Finally, the two institutions carried out a joint study to determine the usefulness of remote-sensing observations (from planes or satellites) to detect new geothermal fields or determine the size of those that have already been discovered.

In the area of geochemistry, the institute has been equipped to analyze and interpret geochemical data obtained from geothermal exploration and thereby characterize potential fields and track their exploration history. Under a contract with the Latin American Energy Organization, thermal anomalies in Guatemala, Nicaragua, Jamaica, Haiti, the Dominican Republic, Peru, and Ecuador have been geochemically interpreted. In regard to prefeasibility and feasibility studies related to geothermal exploration, the IIE is able to sample and perform chemical and isotopic analyses of fluids from natural emanations, as well as chemical and mineralogical analyses of associated solid deposits. It is also able to geochemically interpret data in order to locate high temperature zones and identify the mixing of subterranean fluids. A contract of mutual assistance has been signed with the U.S. Geological Survey to carry out research related to these activities. The laboratories, essential to the performance of these activities, are located in Cuernavaca, Cerro Prieto, and Los Azufres.

FIELD DEVELOPMENT

The IIE has recently acquired the capacity to study problems associated with drilling muds, cement, and corrosion and scale in pipelines and to determine the physical properties of the country rocks to be used in numeric models for reservoir engineering and analysis of well tests. Efforts have been initiated toward the application of complex mathematical simulations of fields.

Under a contract with the commission, the physical, chemical, and rheologic properties of drilling muds used in some of the Los Azufres wells have been monitored in an attempt to correlate the deterioration of the wells with operational problems. An effort has been made to solve these problems by seeking materials that resist conditions present during drilling; cement is one such material. Besides laboratory tests, an analysis of field tests at the bottom of the well has been conducted in conjunction with the commission, the Brookhaven National Laboratory, the U.S. National Bureau of Standards, and various research institutes such as the Southwest Research Institute and private well cementing companies such as Halliburton in order to determine American Petroleum Institute (API) standards of geothermal cement.

A diagnostic study of the corrosion of well pipelines at the Cerro Prieto field is also being carried out under contract with the commission in order to determine the type of corrosion, its cause, and what materials are best to resist it. At the same time, a study is being conducted to identify and evaluate the scale that forms in the pipelines, which tends to block them and to decrease the output of the water-steam mixture from the well.

With regard to reservoir engineering (i.e., the modeling of the field under various conditions and rates of exploitation), a significant effort has been made to create an adequate infrastructure to support the commission. These activities have had considerable support from personnel of the Department of Petroleum and Geothermal Engineering of Stanford University, with whom a contract has been signed. A simulator of the physical conditions of the field has just been installed to measure the physical properties of cores obtained in drilling. These data, detailing permeability, porosity, compressibility, and thermal conductivity, will later be used to create numeric models of the field.

The capacity to analyze test results, including pressure increase and decrease and interference tests, from the field wells has also been developed. These are important in terms of the useful information provided on well conditions and various properties of the field such as transmissibility and the existence of flow barriers. In addition, the flow in the same well under different operational conditions can be numerically simulated by the institute.

The ability to conduct and interpret tests using downhole tracers in the wells is being developed in order to detect high-permeability pathways between wells, which is important for reinjection purposes as well as to provide information that is useful in measuring reserves. Work has been started on complex numeric simulations used to quantify reserves and optimize exploitation.

Several capabilities of the institute relate to the identification of resources and the tracking of exploitation history by geochemical and petrographic methods. Chemical and isotopic analyses of geothermal fluids and chemical and mineralogical analyses of drill cuttings can be conducted. The resulting information is then interpreted to create a geochemical-hydrological model that may indicate the zone of recharge, the general direction of subsurface flow, the possible mixing of geothermal fluid with adjacent cold aquifers, the possible existence of two or more aquifers in one field or of different thermodynamic systems in one field, and the location of the heat source.

EXPLOITATION AND THE GENERATION OF ELECTRICAL POWER

Most efforts by the IIE have gone into the areas of exploitation and the generation of electrical power. This covers everything from basic engineering and associated studies to research in alternative processes for using geothermal energy to generate electricity.

Because each geothermal field has its own particular physical and chemical properties, the design of the installations must be tailored to the characteristics of each site to be optimal. For this reason, the institute has been involved in the basic engineering of plants and the detailed engineering of some unconventional processes.

Under a contract with the commission, the basic engineering of the low-pressure unit 5 of Cerro Prieto I has been completed, as well as detailed engineering of the evaporation plant. This unit has 30 MW of power generated by steam in two stages of evaporation at medium (50 psig) and low pressure (21 psig), using the residual brine from the original stages of evaporation that supplied steam to units 1, 2, 3, and 4 of Cerro Prieto I. The addition of the fifth unit increased the energy efficiency of the field by 20 percent, and it should be noted that no other wells were drilled to install this unit. Furthermore, the commission has completed the basic engineering of the Cerro Prieto II and III plants. Each plant has two 110 MW units with mixed-pressure turbines.

The commission obtained advice from the institute in the evaluation of contract bids for the 5 MW wellhead plants at the Los Azufres field and in specific technical issues such as the drafting and designing of the mixture conduction pipelines. The infrastructure developed in this area was such that the Stone and Webster company contracted the institute as the principal consultant for its bid in the competition to construct the geothermal-electric plant in Miravalle, Costa Rica.

Another job undertaken has been the preparation of design manuals for these installations, since there was no published information on the new components. The first phase focused on the design of Webre-type separators and evaporators (an original New Zealand design). There was no way to predict the efficiency of this equipment nor was it known in quantitative terms what influence the equipment would have on the behavior of various parameters. Generally speaking, the experience and inclinations of the designer have a great influence on the design.

The same uncertainty is evident in regard to the steam silencers used in the regulating system that supplies steam to the turbine according to power demands. It is not possible to regulate the steam in every well and in the brine-steam silencers placed at the wellhead so that the well's output can be released into the atmosphere when need arises. Semitheoretical methods are being developed in these projects to deal with these deficiencies and facilitate the design of these types of installations for the commission.

Pipes designed to conduct the flow in two phases are not common; although there is sufficient information on the conduction of fluids in two phases when the pipes are placed vertically, there is very little information available when the pipes are placed at any other angle. Based on experiments carried out in the Cerro Prieto field, theoretical analyses have validated, thus permitting the design of this latter form of pipe. Due to the importance of pipe angle and flow in field installations, a specially designed fluid mechanics laboratory will be installed in the Cerro Prieto field as a test platform, in order to provide more in-depth study of the behavior of fluids composed of two phases in their movement through different types of equipment used in the geothermal-electric plants.

Because certain operational conditions of field installations can be dangerous and because of the convenience of having more information on the plant's operation, a system to measure various functional parameters has been designed for the Los Azufres field. A typical example of a factor that must be monitored is the level of brine in the separator: under abnormal conditions steam can contain high levels of brine damaging to the turbine. Monitoring also includes the use of remote terminals that centralize the information by area and are connected to a control center where information is stored and processed. The construction of the monitoring installation is currently being studied by the commission.

A major technical problem related to the operation of geothermal electric plants is that scale forms because of the high salt concentration in the fluid extracted from the subsoil. When steam and gases dissolved in it are separated from the fluid, the concentration of brine increases whereas its temperature decreases. These physical and chemical changes affect the chemical equilibrium of salts dissolved in the fluid, which in turn affects the balance of the system. As a result, some compounds precipitate out and form scale on the walls of the pipes or the container that holds them, whereas others remain in suspension. The scale on the walls of the equipment reduces the plants' operating efficiency since that equipment must be periodically taken out of service to be cleaned.

Under a contract with the commission, the institute has developed methodology to prevent and eliminate scale through field research carried out in Cerro Prieto, where fluids with the highest silica content to date have been handled. Chemical and mechanical removal, the kinetics of silica polymerization with changing pH levels, and the use of inhibitors have been studied. There is now sufficient knowledge to define operating pressures in low-pressure evaporators in order to minimize this problem, and there are pilot plants and laboratories in Cerro Prieto to carry out experiments.

Waste fluids from the geothermal plants must be handled in such a way as to avoid environmental pollution. Reinjecting brine into the field is one option that has the additional advantage of both thermally and hydraulically recharging the field. The brine, which has a high silica and total solids content, must be treated to eliminate excesses from over saturation before it is reinjected, since undesirable scale may form in the pipelines and permeability in the field may be damaged. The institute has experimented with some treatments and has determined the most economical method for Cerro Prieto, which is planned for use on a commercial scale.

The recovery of salts contained in the residual brine is another method of environmental control in geothermal fields. As an additional advantage, the recovery of salts (such as potassium chloride, which is used as a fertilizer in agriculture) and lithium chloride (a strategic material used in nuclear fusion reactors) has important economic returns.

In this regard, the institute is able to determine the technical feasibility and most economic method of salt recovery. The IIE has experience in the operation of pilot separation plants and in the concentration and crystallization of salts using solar evaporation tanks. For example, the institute designed and constructed a pilot plant to extract potassium chloride at Cerro Prieto, with evaporation tanks that can yield a half ton per day. On the basis of results obtained in that plant, Fertilizers of Mexico decided to install a potassium chloride extraction plant capable of yielding 80,000 tons per year at Cerro Prieto. This plant is now being designed and built, and when completed, will satisfy a high percentage of the national need for this fertilizer.

Various methods of eliminating hydrogen sulfide in brine produced by wells are currently being technically and economically evaluated. Part of this gas remains dissolved in the brine, but a large part is released and mixes with the steam. Studies carried out at Cerro Prieto show that this does not pose any environmental problem, since concentrations in the surrounding areas are below that specified by law. The evaluation is being done because other geothermal fields in the center of the country are located closer to highly populated areas where the problem may need to be solved.

Under a contract with the commission, a computerized system (SICEP) was designed and put into operation to collect, store, and reproduce technical data gathered at the Cerro Prieto field. Information to be stored includes geologic, geochemical, geophysical, and thermodynamic data obtained during drilling, stimulation, heating, development, operation, and repair of wells, as well as data and specifications of materials, accessories, parts, and equipment used in drilling, completing, maintenance, and repair of the field. This system has a limited capacity to process these data in order to produce graphs, statistics on behavior, and some specific technical calculations according to the needs of the different groups associated with the operaton of the field.

Comparative studies have been carried out on the efficiency of various types of energy conversion processes that transform geothermal energy into electrical power, e.g., evaporation in one, two, or three stages, total flow, binary cycle, and hybrid systems. The hybrid systems, such as binary evaporation, are in general the most efficient.

Because of the apparently large number of low-enthalpy geothermal fields, as well as the possible use of energy contained in residual fluids, the commission instructed the institute to evaluate problems in the use of the binary cycle to generate electricity. Two pilot plants of 10 and 50 KW (kilowatts) are currently in operation at the Los Azufres field. To date, the latter plant has operated using separated steam, but operation using residual brine is planned. The main problem currently being researched involves scale in the heat exchanger. The performance of fluidized bed and direct-contact type exchangers is being compared.

In regard to total flow equipment, support was given to the commission during the test of one of these devices (owned by the International Energy Agency) at the Cerro Prieto field. Observations of the behavior of the machine in operation were analyzed and results showed that it operates satisfactorily under the conditions to which it was exposed, although it is possible to optimize the design in order to improve operational indices and characteristics.

The future of Mexico's geothermal program is closely linked to the plans of the Federal Commission of Electricity concerning the use of geothermal energy. The program is promising in terms of the new challenges it presents and the large amount of work that lies ahead.

7
Experiences of the First Mexican Nuclear Plant at Laguna Verde

Rogelio Ruiz

In this chapter, a general analysis is made of the basic considerations that led the Mexican government to decide to install the first nuclear power plant in Mexico, as well as the problems that arose during its construction and the results achieved to date. The author maintains that the problems of Laguna Verde have their roots in domestic and foreign factors that were not considered when the decision was made. For this reason, the evaluation of the Laguna Verde project to date has been negative.

BACKGROUND TO NUCLEAR DEVELOPMENT IN MEXICO

As in many other countries, interest in Mexico's undertaking a nuclear development program originated in the great expectations generated by the peaceful use of atomic energy, inspired by the Atoms for Peace Program (1953) and the International Conference on the Peaceful Use of Atomic Energy (1955).

The influence of U.S. President Dwight Eisenhower's nuclear policy was felt in the first half of the 1950s by members of the technical staff in the power industry and scientists at the Universidad Nacional Autonomous de Mexico (UNAM). These groups began to promote the idea of Mexico's involvement in the development of the peaceful use of atomic energy. The first steps were taken in the direction of manpower training in the nuclear field. To this end, financial support for international cooperation in the development of atomic energy was made available by several groups, such as the Fund for Peaceful Atomic Development, Inc., founded in Detroit, Michigan, in 1954.[1] In Mexico, this organization, together with the Mexican Light and Power Company, a subsidiary of a private U.S. company, undertook the task of organizing lectures on atomic energy for business leaders and scientists. The University of Michigan also established a grant program for Mexican students of nuclear engineering.

In 1955, the Mexican Light and Power Company successfully realized two important projects: the foundation of an atomic energy library and the Atomic Energy Study Group, composed of engineers from the company itself and others from different organizations.

In August of that year, Mexico sent a group of representatives to the International Conference on the Peaceful Use of Atomic Energy in Geneva, Switzerland, organized by the United States and England, in which approximately seventy nations participated. Several months later, on December 19, 1955, the Mexican government issued a law creating the National Commission of Nuclear Energy (CNEN), a move consistent with the world trend toward the creation of government agencies responsible for nuclear development engendered by the Geneva conference. A group of distinguished physicists from the UNAM were invited to form CNEN, while continuing research and teaching activities at the university. As a result of the heterogeneous nature of the specializations among CNEN members, a series of nuclear programs was drawn up that had very little to do with nuclear energy and was totally divorced from the country's needs. As one researcher has pointed out, "one program was dedicated to space and another to genetic studies,"[2] both of questionable relevance to Mexico's immediate power generation needs.

Despite the diverse nature of these programs, the real legacy of CNEN was the training, both in Mexico and abroad, of a small group of advanced specialists in the nuclear field and other related areas. In addition, CNEN was a pioneer in exploring sections of Mexico in search of potentially productive uranium deposits. At the beginning of the 1970s, the specialists trained with CNEN's assistance attempted to design and build a research reactor in order to advance technological capacity and develop nuclear power in Mexico. The authorities rejected this proposal on the grounds that it would be more economical to buy a TRIGA research reactor (which could later be used as one of the basic research tools in the CNEN's Salazar Nuclear Center).[3]

THE DECISION TO BUILD THE FIRST NUCLEAR POWER PLANT: LAGUNA VERDE

In 1966, the Mexican Federal Commission of Electricity (CFE) decided to enter the field of nuclear power and carried out superficial economic analyses that suggested that the nuclear power option would be competitive with other sources of electricity. When the Diaz Orgaz administration agreed to consider feasibility studies for 500 megawatt (MW) nuclear power plants, the CFE established a nuclear division made up of three professionals who had been trained in nuclear engineering abroad with

CNEN manpower training sources. This group was established as part of the CFE, with the support of internationally famous Mexican scientists, such as Nabor Carrillo and Manuel Sandoval Vallarta. These men, who had promoted the nuclear power project within the government, made an agreement with the Stanford Research Institute in California to prepare a model for analyzing expansion of power systems, to include nuclear power facilities as a potential means for generating power. Technical experts from Petroleos Mexicanos (PEMEX) and the CNEN directly participated in the preparation of this model, as well as officials from the Banco de Mexico and the Nacional Financiera who indirectly contributed by suggesting ideas. Data for the analysis were furnished by the International Atomic Energy Agency (IAEA), the United States Atomic Energy Commission (AEC), and several nuclear power plant construction companies.[4] The results of this analysis indicated that cost was the major factor that would determine the approval of the project establishing a nuclear power plant. It was concluded that "given a 7 percent rise in the price of fuel oil and gas,"[5] the cost of generating power in nuclear and conventional fossil-fuel plants would be the same in terms of investment and operation.

Given the characteristics of the nuclear power plant market, the analysis made the basic recommendation that firm bids for the contract to build a nuclear power plant be requested in order to obtain reliable information on the size of the investment required and the initial generating costs.[6] Following this recommendation, in 1969, prequalification was begun of those manufacturers interested in participating in competitive bidding. The selection was made by a special group made up of members of the CFE and CNEN under the technical guidance of the U.S. firm Burns and Rowe. Although the group had decided to open bidding to nine vendors, only seven firms submitted bids. These were General Electric, Westinghouse, and Combustion Engineering (USA); Atomic Energy of Canada Limited (Canada); Kraftwerk Union (German Federal Republic); Mitsubishi (Japan); and AseaAtom (Sweden). The specifications that the bids had to meet for a nuclear power plant with a 600,000 KW nominal capacity were prepared immediately. While the competing companies were working on their tenders, a group of employees from the CFE and Burns and Rowe used the preliminary data submitted to prepare basic designs for four types of reactors included in the bidding: pressurized water (PWR), boiling water (BWR), advanced gas (AGR), and Candu. According to a national expert, the selection procedure would consider the analysis of the total capital costs of nuclear steam systems in each bid. Then, bids for turbine generators would be added to these costs, so that the latter plus the operating costs over a thirty-year period could be evaluated and divided by the present value of the total power generation estimated for the useful life of each type of plant. The basic criterion for evaluating the bids was the lowest price per kilowatt hour (kWh) unit produced during the operation of the system.[7] After the bids were submitted, each was checked against the corresponding design to determine the total cost of each plant. This evaluation procedure produced two leaders, whose bids were then reevaluated. The best offer was that of Combustion Engineering. However, the entire competitive bidding process was invalidated a short time later.

President Gustavo Diaz Ordaz continued to regard the efforts displayed by proponents of nuclear development with favor. Still he hesitated to define the development of nuclear power. By the mid-1970s, at the president's request, a working group was formed to determine the benefit of continuing studies on the installation of the first nuclear power plant and to prepare a statement to this effect. The group was composed of technical experts from the Secretaria de la Presidencia, Secretaria de Hacienda y Credito Publico, Secretaria de Industria y Comercio, Secretaria de Patrimonio Nacional, and the Secretaria de Relaciones Exteriores as well as the CFE, PEMEX, and the CNEN. All this occurred at a time when the shortfall in domestic oil production made it necessary to import crude, and Mexico's energy shortage was the topic of the day.[8]

On July 16, 1970, a few days before the end of the six-year presidential term, the group submitted its statement on a program for utilizing nuclear energy in Mexico. This concluded with three basic suggestions.

1. Mexico should begin to utilize nuclear energy for generating electric power.
2. The CFE should take advantage of the competitive bidding procedure already held for the equipment for a 660,000 KW capacity nuclear power plant.
3. The experiences derived from the installation of the first nuclear power plant should be systematically evaluated by the federal government to determine the prospects for a greater utilization of nuclear energy.

This statement was based on the implications of three basic criteria and nine considerations as the general frame of reference, which we shall attempt to compare with subsequent policies and results. The three basic criteria used to substantiate the statement were:

1. The rational use of national energy resources according to their availability and output.
2. The timely, adequate, and economical satisfaction of the electrical power demand.
3. The impact of importing equipment and materials on the balance of payments.

The basic considerations used by the group can be summarized.

1. *Satisfying the demand for electricity:* The need to cover the demand for 800,000 KW per year for the interconnected systems of southern Mexico alone, beginning in 1975.

2. *Substituting nuclear materials for hydrocarbons:* Since additional hydroelectric resources capable of producing in the short term were scarce, thermoelectric plants would be required to produce more. This meant higher natural gas and fuel oil requirements. Consequently, hydrocarbons would have to be saved to meet the estimated demand of 26 million barrels in 1971 and 95 million in 1980, which would be consumed in the generation of electrical power. The latter figure represented 37 percent of the total industrial fuel demand forecast by PEMEX. The proposed nuclear power plant would allow for the substitution of 8 million barrels of fuel oil per year.

3. *Investment costs of the nuclear plant:* Investment costs of the nuclear power plant were approximately 60 percent higher than those of an equivalent conventional thermoelectric plant. However, over a thirty-year period of operation, the lower fuel costs for the former made total generating costs practically the same for the two types of plants. Considering the trend in the relative costs of fossil and nuclear fuels, the group thought the nuclear plants would probably be more economical than plants using fossil fuels for generating power. Moreover, the price of fuel oil paid by the CFE was 117.50 pesos per cubic meter, f.o.b. point of embarkation, whereas the average price paid by the rest of the industry was 141.96 pesos. In addition, the group expressed the opinion that nuclear fuel costs would tend to decline or, at least, remain constant.

4. *The availability of better methods of financing the nuclear option:* Arrangements for financing for the nuclear plant proposed to CFE were better than those available for conventional plants.

5. *The additional amount of investment in comparison with a conventional plant:* The group considered that the additional investment in the nuclear power plant, as compared with conventional thermoelectric plants that would be replaced by the former, would result in an average increase of less than 3 percent in the CFE's investment program from 1971 to 1975, the duration of the construction period of the nuclear plant.

6. *The impact of the nuclear option on the balance of payments:* The group considered that the import factor for the nuclear power plant was greater than for conventional power plants. However, if the fuel costs for the nuclear power plant were taken into account, the impact on the balance of payments would be similar to that of installing a conventional plant. On the other hand, it was pointed

out that the fuel oil that was saved by the nuclear power plant could be exported at an attractive price in foreign currency and this would favor the nation's balance of payments.

7. *Promoting the development of greater technological integration:* The group considered that using nuclear plants to generate electricity would permit the utilization of an, as yet untapped, energy resource, and encourage the development of uranium mining. In the future, this would bring about a greater integration in the manufacture of nuclear fuels and plant components.

8. *Guaranteeing the enrichment and supply of Mexican uranium:* The group believed in the possibility of ensuring the enrichment of Mexican uranium through an agreement with the International Atomic Energy Agency, thus eliminating the need to enter into bilateral agreements with countries possessing uranium enrichment technology.

9. *Support for the peaceful development of nuclear energy:* It was thought that the establishment of the first nuclear power plant would demonstrate Mexico's interest in the peaceful use of nuclear energy and that this would, in turn, be an expression of consistency with the country's position in support of the Treaty of Tlatelolco.

Almost at the same time that the working group was presenting these suggestions, the results of evaluating the bids submitted by technological firms were sent to President Diaz Ordaz. The president decided to leave the final decision to his successor, in view of the imminent change of administrations. On January 31, 1971, the new president, Luis Echeverria, held a work session with the Secretaries of Treasury, the Presidency, and Industry and Trade as well as the Directors of the Bank of Mexico and the CFE, the Under-Secretary of Foreign Relations, and officials from other agencies. At this meeting, Echeverria called for the presentation of the project designed to establish the first nuclear power plant and gave instructions for the formation of a subgroup to reanalyze the problem from a financial point of view and in terms of substitute energy sources. This subgroup was composed of the Presidency's Directors of Public Investment and Economic Studies, the Director of Treasury Studies within the Ministry of Treasury, the General Director of Electric Power within the Ministry of Industry and Trade, the advisor to the Secretary of Treasury and the Head of the CFE's Power Industry Research Institute. At the time that this subgroup was formed, some of the most important problems had already been solved.[9]

The majority of financial agreements had already been made. The World Bank had shown interest in granting credit to cover a sizeable portion of the investment in the nuclear power plant by means of a long-term credit of $41,280,000 for supplementary equipment and part of the construction work. In addition, there was a possibility of an additional credit of $11,600,000 which would be earmarked for acquiring the first fuel charge. The Export-Import Bank of the United States had offered $34,240,000 and the Export Bank of Japan, $9,760,000. It was also expected that financing could be obtained for foreign transportation, and, in that case, only $29,600,000 would have to be spent by Mexico during the five years required to build the nuclear power plant. Comparative analyses revealed to the group that constructing the plant would not significantly affect the country's foreign debt. What would be considered Mexico's share in the financing would be covered by the CFE's investment program for the 1971-1976 six-year period, which amounted to $2,400 million. It was estimated that the cost of the nuclear plant would be $128 million including the first fuel charge. Also, the argument was offered that this plant would substitute for the equivalent capacity of conventional thermal plants that cost approximately $76 million. Therefore, the additional net investment would only be 2 or 3 percent of the CFE's total investment program.

The International Atomic Energy Agency had already approved the site chosed for the installation of the nuclear power plant (Laguna Verde, Veracruz) after having examined all of the siting studies. In the latter, seven locations that fulfilled the requirements for nuclear plants were examined, and the costs of construction, operation, and transportation of energy to the electric systems were analyzed.

PEMEX's representative stressed the benefit that would be derived from having CFE's demand depend on sources other than supply of industrial fossil fuels. In this way, PEMEX could make its future allotments without the commitment of first satisfying the CFE's requirements. In addition, the CFE was committed to look for alternate energy sources since the 1971 Statement indicated that if the CFE failed to do so, the fuel subsidy given to the power industry would continue to directly affect PEMEX's finances. In order to significantly influence CFE's demand, PEMEX would have to increase fuel prices for thermoelectric plants on a par with the current average price in force among industrial consumers. Once the price was increased, PEMEX thought that a positive effect would be felt on the economy of nuclear plants, making them just as, if not more, economical as compared with thermoelectric plants.

On February 11, 1971, the second intergovernmental group established to evaluate the factors involved in the installation of the first Mexican nuclear power plant concluded that: (1) from the point of view of domestic energy economy, the nuclear plant should be constructed immediately, in order to take advantage of the competitive bidding contest that had been held, since the term of the bids expired that month; (2) the status of preliminary work (quotation, site selection, preliminary design, position of the World Bank, etc.) would make it possible for the plant to begin commercial operations by May 1976; and (3) for Laguna Verde to be more than an isolated effort, the group of evaluators suggested the beginning of national energy planning as soon as possible, since this would permit, among other things, the establishment of a more consistent policy for the construction of subsequent nuclear power facilities.[10]

Despite the revalidation of the Laguna Verde project by the Echeverria administration, several issues involved in the political advantages and disadvantages of the light water reactor (LWR) favored in the first bidding analysis had to be reconsidered. The second evaluating committee, which represented different interests, questioned the compatibility of the requirements of the light water reactor with the nation's interest in maintaining independence in energy matters. The arguments emphasized the problems resulting from contracting technology that required uranium enrichment. The latter would require Mexico to depend on foreign sources for the atomic fuel supply needed for the plant. There was also disagreement among the group members as to whether light water reactor technology would be obsolete by the time the nuclear plant began operating. Several of the evaluators, especially those from the Instituto Nacional de Energia Nuclear, were also concerned with the failure to consider domestic participation in the construction of the first nuclear power plant during the analysis of the bids. The ability of CFE to carry out the nuclear power project without major difficulties was also questioned, as was the positive impact that the project would have on the nation's scientific development. Despite disagreement on basic issues involved in the decision, the evaluating subgroup decided not to delay the initiation of the Laguna Verde project any longer. Competitive bidding was reopened. However, on this occasion Atomic Energy of Canada decided to withdraw as a result of the supposed partiality shown toward the U.S. bidders, Burns and Rowe, in evaluating tenders. By May 1972, it was resolved that General Electric would supply a boiling water reactor (BWR) and Mitsubishi, the turbine generator. All competing tenders attempted to satisfy one of the most important bidding requirements, which was the effective transfer of the part of the technology associated with the nuclear fuel cycle. As an immediate step, the effective transfer of information necessary for the eventual fabrication of fuel in Mexico was promised, and, in September 1972, letters of intent were signed for the first unit with equipment procurers, leaving open the option for contracting the second unit.

By 1973, the CFE had already done a new study on the advantages of acquiring the second unit for Laguna Verde. However, this was attacked by CFE's Planning and Programming Management Department on the grounds that, in many ways, it would not be cost effective. Despite the recommendation not to acquire this unit, an agreement was signed for it with suppliers in August 1973.

In Mexico, one of the factors that greatly influenced the decision to build a nuclear power plant was the participation of famous Mexican nuclear experts in the international meetings organized by the IAEA. This favored personal contact among technical staff, scientists, and managers from countries that consumed and produced nuclear technology. Also, the former AEC influenced those who formulated the U.S. decision to favor nuclear development in Mexico by spreading information and encouraging participation in joint studies. The result of this policy led Mexico to become involved with the IAEA and the AEC in evaluating the possibility of installing a dual nuclear facility.[11]

Immediately after the type of technology to be used in Laguna Verde was defined, construction work was begun. This gave rise to a whole new series of problems.

THE PROBLEMS OF THE LAGUNA VERDE POWER PLANT

The problems of Laguna Verde can be explored on the basis of the tentative answers to three questions, which will serve as a guide to evaluating the accuracy or inaccurary of the recommendations made by the intergovernmental groups and as a point of interest on the support that was given to the then urgent construction of the nuclear power plant.

In terms of the results achieved and present day events, how valid are the reference criteria and the considerations put forward in the statements made by the two intergovernmental committees? What vicissitudes has the construction of Laguna Verde experienced and what experience has been gained from them to optimized national nuclear development?

The Laguna Verde project has experienced problems of both a domestic and foreign nature. On the domestic front, these difficulties have been mainly political and economic. Politically, the very structure and modus operandi of Mexico's political systems has had a direct impact on Laguna Verde's development. Changes of directors, the closeness or distance of key people to the president of Mexico, internal conflicts within the CFE, and difficulties between CFE and prominent members of the nuclear community or other governmental interest groups are some of the factors that have impeded the smooth functioning of the Laguna Verde project. Several examples will illustrate this point. Shortly after Laguna Verde's technological equipment order was placed, a new director was appointed. The new man felt that there was uncertainty both at home and abroad concerning the project's design, type of reactor, site, construction, and the skills of the project development group. The new director instituted changes that delayed the project almost three years. During President Luis Echeverria's six-year term the management of the CFE changed three times, and there were subsequent changes in manpower and policy. The last of these managements, which was the longest lived, replaced several foreign specialists in charge of critical issues in the design and installation of the Laguna Verde facility with Mexican technical personnel. All that this achieved was a rapid return to the previous situation. The CFE's internal and external political feuds, as they were called by Jose Lopez Portilla in his tour of the agency, and the sequence of hiring-cancelling-rehiring of suppliers and construction personnel have also encouraged the fragmentation of the decision-making process, and, therefore, the increased expense of Laguna Verde.

Other problems followed from these. When President Lopez Portillo's administration took charge of the project, the orginally contracted construction company moved its offices to New York. This caused another considerable delay in the project and seriously hampered possibilities for the rapid transfer of technology. With regard to the economy, the nuclear power facility has suffered from the impact of the processes of inflation, recession, and devaluation that have plagued Mexico in recent years.

The problems that the project has encountered abroad have been political in nature. Variations in the export policies of technology vendors have had considerable impact on the project's conception and implementation. If we add to this the technical problems that have arisen during the construction of the plant itself, it is most probable that Laguna Verde will face licensing problems as a result of changes in some of the original designs and the loss of quality assurance in their construction. When the Laguna Verde units were contracted, it was agreed that licenses would be granted by the vendor's country of origin. Because the design is General Electric Mark II, the decision to authorize the beginning of operations belongs to the United States Nuclear Regulatory Commission (NRC). Several of the key people responsible for the project believe that the most serious problem to be faced will be precisely licensing by U.S. authorities.[12] Laguna Verde has been a negative experience in most of the areas that justified the government's decision to go ahead with the project.

One of the main rationalizations for the decision to install the first nuclear power plant in Mexico was the need to cover the annual electric power demand of the country's southern interconnected systems by 1976. The project has been delayed seven years and will not begin operating until 1985, due to the problems that have already been mentioned and, most of all, to the budget cuts imposed by the government.[13]

The goal of substituting 8 million barrels of fuel oil a year with nuclear materials by start-up (1976), which was an important consideration in the decision to go ahead with the nuclear power facility, has not been met. This will mean a substitution loss of 72 million barrels of fuel oil by the opening of the plant in 1985. The consideration to substitute nuclear materials for hydrocarbons responded to Mexico's 1971 energy needs. However, due to the delay in the operation of the plant and recent discoveries of large hydrocarbon reserves, as well as the escalating costs of nuclear facilities, the substitution of hydrocarbons has been a less pressing objective. The amount and, therefore, the importance of the recently discovered reserves should be underscored. In 1979, annual fuel oil production was 86,684,000 barrels,[14] and in December 1981, proven hydrocarbon reserves rose to 72,008 million barrels. These reserves are composed of 48,084 million barrels of crude (67 percent), 8,915 million barrels of gas liquids (12 percent), and the equivalent of 15,009 million barrels of crude in dry gas (21 percent).[15] Annual gas production during 1981 was 1,482,196 million cubic feet (ft^3) with an average daily production of 4,060.8 million ft^3.[16] At present, 300 million ft^3 are exported daily and this export volume could be increased to 600 million ft^3.[17]

The investment costs of Laguna Verde have escalated considerably due to the increased costs of nuclear power plants and associated facilities, fuel and enrichment costs, and the inflation that has plagued the country for years. In February 1971, the cost of nuclear power plants including the first fuel charge was estimated at $128 million.[18] Four years later this estimate had risen to almost $480 million, and in 1979 the total cost was approximately $1,405 million. No one knows for certain how much the costs will rise by the time the first power plant begins operating, but several figures have been proposed. In December 1981, months before the dramatic 50 percent currency devaluation, one nonofficial estimate placed the costs at $1,830 million.[19] Another figure was $1,525 million.[20] The project manager, Agustin Perez Ruiz, has criticized the arbitrariness of these project cost estimates, for in order to make a realistic estimate it would be necessary to make a study to determine the real value of what has been invested. Nevertheless, the manager points out that, to date, almost $710 million have been invested in Laguna Verde, of which $82 million have been spent in 1982, since it is the CFE's priority project.[21] Surely costs will continue to rise in view of the delays that the plant is experiencing, Mexico's economic recession, and accumulated interest, inasmuch as the plant will begin operating nine years later than scheduled, if no other obstacles intervene. Another factor to be considered in higher operating costs is the increase in the prices of uranium enrichment services, if the present trends continue. The prices since 1973 are noted in Table 7.1.

Table 7.1
Uranium Enrichment Costs (dollars per SWU[a])

1973	$35
1974	$43
1975	$54
1976	$62
1977	$74
1978	$88
1979	$100
1980	$110
1981	--
1982	$139-$159

[a]The uranium enrichment process is measured in separate work units (SWU). Each uranium enrichment reactor, depending on the type, yearly operation, and power, consumes different amounts of SWU per year.

This represents an annual average cost increase of 17 percent, which is considerably higher than the inflationary rate in countries where the process is carried out. In other words, enrichment has become increasingly expensive in real terms at an accelerated rate.[22]

With regard to guaranteeing uranium enrichment and fuel procurement for Laguna Verde through an agreement with the IAEA, several obstacles have been encountered, mainly as a consequence of the limits imposed by the American nuclear nonproliferation policy.

On February 12, 1974, the Mexican government signed two agreements: the Mexico-IAEA bilateral agreement to guarantee that agency's assistance in constructing the first Mexican nuclear power facility at Laguna Verde near Alto Lucero in the state of Veracruz.[23] The second one was a trilateral agreement (Mexico-IAEA-United States) to ensure the supply of enriched uranium. In the latter agreement, the United States AEC, through a cooperation agreement with the IAEA, committed itself to supply the agency with enriched uranium for the first Laguna Verde unit. This agreement was implemented in a long-term contract that specified the particular terms and conditions for the supply of uranium enrichment services (a procedure by which uranium is physically altered to obtain a richer mixture of the fissionable isotope, uranium 235), including prices and advance payment.[24]

Four months after the first trilateral agreement was signed, on June 14, 1974, another agreement was concluded, which contained several amendments covering the second half of the Laguna Verde project, according to a decision by the Mexican government.[25] On August 31, 1977, General Electric requested a license from the U.S. government to export 9,691 kilograms (kg) of uranium 235, contained in 377,600 kg of uranium dioxide and enriched to a maximum of 4 percent, in strict compliance with the aforementioned agreements.

The uranium dioxide with a low enrichment level would be processed and assembled, to be used as the first fuel charge for Laguna Verde reactors 1 and 2. Initially each unit would be charged with 444 packages of fuel rods containing 81,000 kg of uranium.[26] The first shipment was scheduled for December 1978, upon or after the issuance of the export license.

When General Electric's request reached the U.S. State Department, an investigation was made to determine whether the application complied with the export policies for nuclear material specified in the cooperation agreement between the IAEA and the United States. This investigation revealed that the Mexican government had met all the requirements of the trilateral agreement concerning the transfer of technology, and, therefore, the president of the United States recommended that the corresponding license be issued. This recommendation contained two additional considerations that weighed heavily in Mexico's favor. On the one hand, the Special Report on Implementing IAEA Safeguards testified to Mexico's compliance with the safety measures imposed by the agency to guarantee the nonutilization of nuclear materials for military purposes. On the other, Mexico had played an active and constructive part in all matters concerning nonproliferation and nuclear disarmament. In addition, Mexico was one of the first countries to ratify the Non-Proliferation Treaty and, perhaps, the most enthusiastic supporter of the Treaty of Tlatelolco. All things considered, Mexico had played an important and influential role among the nonaligned countries belonging to international organizations, such as the IAEA. In view of these facts, the U.S. chief executive recommended that the nuclear fuel export license for Laguna Verde be issued without further delay, due to the special importance that this had for nonproliferation and Mexican-U.S. relations.

Despite this and other recommendations, on January 19, 1978, the United States government temporarily canceled the trilateral commitment (IAEA-Mexico-United States) to supply Mexico with enriched uranium, until such time as Mexico could guarantee to the U.S. government that it would refrain from reprocessing the fuel used in the nuclear power facility. Another condition imposed by the U.S. government required the Mexican government to accept visits, inspection, and direct supervision of the nuclear facility by representatives of the U.S. government. While all this was happening, the U.S. Senate and House of Representatives were studying a proposed bill sent by the president, a bill designed to halt the proliferation of nuclear weapons. Under these circumstances, the fuel request for Laguna Verde was blocked on March 10, 1978, the enactment of President Jimmy Carter's Non-Proliferation Law. When this law was approved, the procedure for the export license and the subsequent fuel delivery to the Mexican government were formally suspended. The new law was applied retroactively, in violation of an international agreement already in effect, and in an attempt to impose supervisory and direct control measures on Mexico's nuclear activities. These measures were more stringent than those established by the IAEA, which has been the main body responsible for ensuring against the proliferation of nuclear weapons.

In reality, the new criteria for exporting nuclear material took effect for Mexico on April 27, 1977, when the proposed bill reached Congress, rather than the date that Congress approved the 1978 Non-Proliferation Law.[27] This is the only explanation for the moratorium in Mexico's enriched uranium export license during the period between the formal request (August 31, 1977) and the approval of the law (March 10, 1978).

National and international reactions to President Carter's Non-Proliferation Law expressed profound rejection. Within the U.S. nuclear industry, Carter's policy was interpreted as an obstacle to exporting and a lack of support for developing improved nuclear technologies. The industry's view can be synthesized in the comments of Dwight Porter, U.S. ambassador to the IAEA and an employee of Westinghouse in Washington, D.C.: "The Carter Administration has never lent its support to nuclear exports and is just slightly less than hostile to them."[28] Porter also complained that the export license for the sale of a nuclear reactor for a power plant in the Philippines "was pigeonholed in the State Department while the approval of the sale of non-nuclear materials for the same plant was being delayed in the Department of Commerce." In addition, he added that "in my opinion, this is an example of the paralysis operating within this Administration, rather than the result of a political decision."[29] In the United States, the majority of criticism of Carter's nonproliferation policy pointed out the negative effect that it would have on the already dramatic conditions existing within the U.S. nuclear industry with regard to new orders. Dissenters accused the president and Congress of creating an atmosphere of uncertainty and resentment in the nuclear community with the new regulations on nuclear exports.[30]

Mexico's reaction to the Carter nonproliferation policy was also negative, as was that of many other Third World countries with developing or operating nuclear programs, on the grounds that it was a unilateral policy that violated already established agreements for technology transfer critical to the peaceful use of nuclear energy. The Mexican press echoed the government's official position and the irritated criticisms of U.S. nuclear policy made by leaders of public opinion and syndicates in the Mexican power industry. There were even those who interpreted the application of Carter's nuclear policy to Mexico as a way of pressuring for a larger volume and better prices in the sale of Mexican natural gas to the United States.[31]

Mexico's reply was so vehement more because of the U.S. violation of the practices established by the international community and commitments assumed by that government when the 1968 Non-Proliferation Treaty was signed[32] than because of the possible harm to Laguna Verde through a revision of the fuel procurement agreements for the power plant. There had already been a two-year construction delay and, therefore, the plant was not in condition to "receive" the enriched uranium.

In the face of Mexico's reply to the possible application of the provisions of Carter's nuclear law, on December 29, 1978, Under Secretary of State Louis V. Nosenzo sent a memorandum to James R. Shea, a Nuclear Regulatory Commission official, urging him to issue Mexico's enriched uranium export license and pointing out that if the delay extended beyond December 31, 1978, the CFE would have to pay from $30,000 to $40,000 per month for fuel storage as of that date. This would decidely affect U.S.-Mexican relations as well as Mexico's support for joint nonproliferation measures.[33]

The U.S. State Department's petition to the Nuclear Regulatory Commission was based on its own analysis, which pointed out that, according to the 1978 Non-Proliferation Law, Mexico had complied with all the requirements for the export of nuclear materials specified in the 1954 Atomic Energy Law,[34] amended in 1978. Therefore, exporting nuclear fuel to Mexico would not constitute a threat to the defense and security of the United States. Moreover, the export license fully complied with the terms of the cooperation agreement between the United States and the IAEA. Mexico, in turn, respected the spirit and letter of both the trilateral cooperation agreements and the nuclear cooperation agreement project with the IAEA.[35]

On January 4, 1979, the U.S. State Department sent another memorandum to the Nuclear Regulatory Commission, pressuring once again for the prompt issuance of the license in question. Finally, on January 14, 1979, after the commission had again verified Mexico's compliance with all export license requirements, and even its overcompliance with the physical safety measures required by the IAES, and in view of the urgency expressed by the U.S. State Department and the Mexican government, General Electric was granted the license to export fuel for the first charge and five additional charges at Laguna Verde.[36]

Another important argument in favor of the Laguna Verde decision was that prompting greater technological integration through the installation of a nuclear power plant would favor domestic fabrication of certain capital goods for the power industry. This would encourage independent industrialization and contribute to generating employment, overcoming the trade deficit, raising the technological level, and vertically and horizontally integrating Mexican industry.[37]

In certain technical circles, the viewpoint has been expressed that the learning costs of Laguna Verde must be accepted. It is argued, and not without foundation, that this kind of experience costs the country very dearly, since Mexican-built equipment will have a higher price than equipment acquired abroad on a "turnkey" basis. However, the additional argument is offered that Laguna Verde will enable Mexico to make technological progress toward greater integration and independence and, finally, to produce more highly sophisticated equipment for the future development of a nuclear power program.

What has the real experience been in this regard? Domestic production has not been able to satisfy, even minimally, the bulk of Laguna Verde's major technological requirements due to the enormous technical problems that must be solved. One of these problems is related to a more general difficulty of the Mexican capital goods industry, in which slowdowns are seen in materials and laboratory testing at the beginning and end of the equipment production cycle. As a result of the foregoing, many domestic manufacturing problems have to do with processing imported components that are then returned to the country of origin for finishing and testing.[38]

The assistant manager of Evaluation and Economic Studies at the CFE, Jose Luis Aburto Avila, has indicated that

> in order to get an idea of the complexity of the step to be taken in assimilating high technology, we can compare one characteristic, the economic life of the equipment which is presently manufactured in Mexico, with that of equipment to be manufactured in the future. A car motor has an economic life of between 7,000 and 12,000 hours, whereas another piece of rotary equipment, a turbogenerator, has an economic life of between 130,000 and 170,000 hours, or 15 times greater. This fact places considerable demands on the quality of materials and manufacturing processes. Meeting them required solid, well-conceived and executed projects which have the active participation of the government, the power industry, and national manufacturers[39] [within a context, we might add, of scientific and technological policy that favors the mastery and sustained development

of highly complex technologies].

The concept of integrated nuclear technology is based on a series of assumptions that have not as yet been totally carried out. One of the latter is that nuclear technology is available to any purchaser, just like any other type of merchandise. The fact is that those who possess this technology are faced with the dilemma of how to promote it without encouraging its spread and, therefore--they argue--the proliferation of nuclear weapons. In an attempt to solve this incompatibility of objectives, very strict or fairly strict policies for the transfer of technology have been implemented as the case required. In addition, several attempts have been made at establishing cartels for technology and nuclear fuels, as in the case of the London Club. From time to time, the results of these measures have inhibited the international flow of nuclear technology.

The domestic integration of nuclear technology is conditioned by social, economic, technological, and political factors existing both at home and abroad. With regard to the social factors, Mexico does not yet have the "critical mass" of manpower to carry out basic and applied research on the nuclear technologies of major importance. In the economic sphere, integration meets with tremendous competition from other national priorities requiring substantial capital investment. The installation of a nuclear power plant calls for very high capital costs for the producer countries and even higher costs for the developing countries that import the facilities or attempt to substitute for them gradually. Excessive amounts are spent on import substitution projects in which more is paid for imported components and foreign debt service fees, associated with the purchase of equipment partially manufactured in Mexico, than would be paid for directly importing the entire equipment with supplier financing. The country's foreign exchange balance becomes even more negative if the imports required by domestic manufacturers are taken into account.[40]

CONCLUSIONS

The fundamental criteria and considerations that warranted the installation of the first nuclear power plant in Mexico have been invalidated by experience. The basic objective of Laguna Verde, the timely, adequate, and economical satisfaction of part of the electric power demand, will not be met since the plant will begin operating after a nine-year delay and with increased real installation and operating costs.

To date, the results of the first Mexican nuclear power project have been negative. This can be explained by the simple fact that it was conceived within a social, technical, and political context that is still far from able to realize this type of project in the best possible way. The project arose in a period in which the country was experiencing a shortage of energy, as well as technological and financial resources, manpower, and infrastructure, which doomed the timely satisfaction of the power demand to failure in advance. The project was initiated under the auspices of its domestic and foreign proponents without the proper organization, without the integrated evaluation of alternative energy sources and open technologies for Mexico, without a realistic inventory of domestic capacity to reasonably guarantee a minimum of success, and, fundamentally, without an awareness that the installation of a nuclear power facility implies complications that cannot be solved with improvisation nor with the rhythms and habits dictated by the political vicissitudes of contemporary Mexico.

The attempt to incorporate nuclear technology as a tool for national development has been hasty and disruptive to the economy of the power industry and to the national economy as well. Officially, the expenditure for the Laguna Verde project to date is 33 billion pesos at current prices. In terms of 1971 prices, this would represent about three times the total costs initially estimated. It should be pointed out that this estimate of expenses is perhaps less than the real total, since it is highly probable that disbursements for certain items have not been included. The lack of detailed information on the payments made during the construction period prevents the total amount of investment from being presented. Therefore, the figures given here are only an approximation.

The results of Laguna Verde are the results of any nuclear project in a developing country with deficiencies similar to Mexico's. Unquestionably, the country has gained experience from having undertaken the construction of a nuclear plant. However, domestic participation is still limited, as a result of the technological, scientific, and manpower deficiencies discussed herein. Thus Laguna Verde has become the focus of urgent and profound reflection on the benefits of formulating national nuclear programs whose goals far exceed the means at the country's disposal.

NOTES

1. The activities of this organization included nuclear research and the publication and distribution of information on the peaceful use of atomic energy through consultancies, technical aid, information for foreign visitors, foreign missions, and support for related organizations in other countries.

2. Antonio Ponce, "Mexico ingreso a ciegas en la

era nuclear" (Mexico has blindly entered the nuclear age), note by F. Pena, *Uno mas Uno* (Mexico City), July 14, 1980.

3. Juan Eibenschutz, "Mexico," in Everett Katz J. and U. Marwah S. Onkar, *Nuclear Power in Developing Countries* (Lexington, MA: Lexington Books, 1982), chapter 13.

4. Ibid., p. 247.

5. "Dictamen sobre la conveniencia de instalar la primera planta nucleoelectrica" (Mexico City: July 16, 1970). Document prepared by technical experts from the Ministries of the Presidency, Treasury, National Resources, Industry and Trade, and Foreign Relations, as well as the Federal Power Commission, the Mexican Oil Company, and the National Energy Commission.

6. Ibid., p. 4.

7. Eibenschutz, op. cit., p. 251.

8. "From 1970 to 1972 crude imports rose substantially to cover the growing shortfall between production and domestic consumption. In 1972 alone, they were 9,986 thousand barrels." Eduardo Turrent Diaz, *La industria petrolera mexicana, 1965-1973,* thesis for the Master's Degree in Economics (Mexico City: El Colegio de Mexico, 1976), p. 128 (mimeo.).

9. "Dictamen sobre el proyecto nucleoelectrico de la Comision Federal de Electricidat" (Mexico City: February 11, 1971). Document prepared by Directors of Public Investment and Economic Studies of the Presidency, Director of Treasury Studies of the Ministry of Treasury, Deputy Director of Industrial Production of PEMEX, Director General of Electricity at the Ministry of Industry and Trade, the Advisor to the Minister of Treasury, and the Head of the CFE's Electrical Industry Research Institute. (This document will be referred to hereafter as the 1971 Statement.)

10. Ibid., p. 3.

11. Eibenschutz, op. cit., p. 248.

12. Ibid., p. 254.

13. Jose Andres de Oteyza, "En Laguna Verde us habra operaciones hasta 1985," note by Marco A. Mares, *Uno mas Uno* (Mexico City), June 26, 1982.

14. Secretaria de Programacion y Buenopuesto, *La industria petrolera en Mexico* (Mexico: 1980).

15. Petroleos Mexicanos (PEMEX), *Memoria de labores* (Mexico: PEMEX, 1981), p. 7.

16. Ibid., p. 79.

17. "Mexico's Expanding Role in World Oil Markets," *Petroleum Intelligence Weekly,* Special Supplement, June 18, 1982.

18. 1971 Statement.

19. "Mil millones de pesos requerira Laguna Verde," *Uno mas Uno* (Mexico City), October 12, 1981.

20. "Cuarento mil millones de pesos, el costo total de la planta de Laguna Verde," note by Humberto Aranda, *Excelsior* (Mexico City), December 16, 1981.

21. "En Laguna Verde disminuyeron hasta 10 por

ciento las obras como onsecuencio de la crisis economica," note by Abelardo Martin, *Uno mas Uno* (Mexico City), July 21, 1982.

22. See Alen J. Large, "Why the Price of Atomic Fuel Keeps Rising," *The Wall Street Journal*, July 2, 1981; and Antonio Ponce, "Energia nuclear, el precio del enriquecimiento," *Uno mas Uno* (Mexico City), April 4, 1982.

23. Three articles of this bilateral agreement are particularly important. Article II requires the IAEA to request the Unites States to transfer and export to Mexico the reactor and its components, as well as spare parts, in accordance with the contract made between Mexico and the U.S. supplier. Article IV mentions the safeguarding measures agreed upon between the IAEA and the Mexican government. In paragraph 1, Mexico agrees that neither the reactor nor the nuclear material contained, used, produced, or processed in or through the use of the reactor will be employed for military purposes. In paragraph 2, the Mexican government commits itself to respect the agreements made with the IAEA concerning the application of the safeguards mentioned in the Treaty for the Prohibition of Nuclear Weapons in Latin America and the Non-Proliferation of Nuclear Weapons Treaty signed on September 27, 1972. See: IAEA, *II. Agreement Between the International Atomic Energy Agency and the Government of the United Mexican States for Assistance by the Agency in Establishing a Nuclear Power Facility*, Doc. INFCIRC/203 (Vienna: IAEA, April 5, 1974).

24. In Article I, paragraph 2, the commission and the Mexican government agreed on two aspects that are basic to the operation of Laguna Verde: (1) a program for uranium enrichment services, specifying the number of separate work units that the commission should supply to Mexico and the delivery date for the former, within a limited time period that would begin in 1976 and end in 1986 and (2) suitable procedures for specifying the amounts and tentative delivery dates for both uranium 238 by Mexico and the weight percentage of uranium 235 by the United States. Article III, paragraph 2, makes reference to the delivery terms for nuclear materials. It is stated herein that arrangements for exporting all materials delivered by the United States Atomic Energy Commission are Mexico's responsibility, with prior approval of all export licenses and permits by the U.S. government. With regard to terminating, suspending, or amending the contract in the long term, it is stipulated that joint notification of any of the former actions should be given to the IAEA and that the parties to the agreement *must consult each other in case of any amendment* (Article VI, paragraph 2; author's italics). See: IAEA, *I. Agreement for the Supply of Uranium Enrichment Services for a Nuclear Power Facility in Mexico*, Doc. INFCIRC/203 (Vienna: IAEA, April 5, 1974), pp. 1,3.

25. IAEA, *Agreement for the Supply of Uranium Enrichment Services for a Second Reactor Unit for a Nuclear Power Facility in*

Mexico, Doc. INFCIRC/203 Add. 1 (Vienna: IAEA, October 31, 1974).

26. Nuclear Regulatory Commission Document XSNM-1194, March 2, 1979.

27. Article IV of this law has been the most problematical for both developed countries and underdeveloped nations with nuclear programs. Several additional requirements are stated herein concerning the approval of export licences for materials and nuclear equipment. In section 404 (a), it is indicated that immediately after the Non-Proliferation Treaty becomes effective, the president must begin a program to renegotiate previous cooperation agreements still in force or, in lieu of this, to obtain the consent of the parties with regard to the requirements to be met in subsequent cooperation agreements within the framework of the 1954 Atomic Energy Law.

28. William J. Lanouette, "U.S. Nuclear Industry Can't Expect Much Help from Abroad," *National Journal*, July 21, 1979, p. 1209.

29. Ibid., P. 1209.

30. John V. Granger, *Technology and International Relations* (San Francisco, CA: W. H. Freeman and Co., 1979), p. 152.

31. "El embargo de uranio, presion de E.U. para comprar gas barato," *El Sol de Mexico* (Mexico City), January 30, 1978.

32. In fact, Article IV, paragraph 1, states that nothing in this treaty should be interpreted as affecting the inalienable rights of the signatory states to develop research, production, and the use of nuclear energy for peaceful purposes, without discrimination, and in compliance with Articles I and II of this treaty. In paragraph 2, it is indicated that "all nations party to the Treaty commit themselves to facilitate and have access to the greatest possible exchange of equipment, materials, and technological and scientific information for the peaceful use of nuclear energy. Parties to the Treaty that are in a position to do so, should cooperate to contribute to the greater development of the peaceful use of nuclear energy, especially in the territory of the signatory States which do not possess nuclear weapons, taking into account the needs of developing areas." See United States, Senate Committee on Governmental Affairs, Joint Committee Print: *Nuclear Proliferation Factbook*, 96th Congress, second session, September 1980, p. 465.

33. Letter from Louis V. Nosenzo, Deputy Assistant Secretary of the State Department, to James R. Shea, Director of the International Program Office of the Nuclear Regulatory Commission (NRC), December 29, 1978.

34. Especially those that are contemplated in sections 126 a (1), 127, and 128 of this law. See United States, Senate Committee on Governmental Affairs, op. cit., pp. 51-57.

35. Ibid.

36. Nuclear Regulatory Commission Document CECY-79-121, February 14, 1979.

37. Eduardo Ibarrola, "La integracion nacional de maqinaria y equipo utilizado por el sector electrico." Paper presented at the ninth roundtable on Energy and Industrialization, *Los Energeticos en la Industrializacion y sus Impactos Regionales*. IEPES, Consulta Popular para la Planeacion de Energeticos y Desarrollo Nacional, Mexico City, May 25, 1982.

38. Jose Luis Aburto Avila, "Costos y beneficios de la fabricacion nacional de maquinaria y equipos para el sector electrico." Paper presented at the ninth roundtable on Energy and Industrialization, *Los Energeticos en la Industrilizacion y sus Impactos Regionales*. IEPES, Consulta Popular para la Planeacion de Energeticos y Desarrollo Nacional, Mexico City, May 25, 1982.

39. Ibid.

40. Ibid.

8
The Mexico-Venezuela Oil Agreement of San Jose: A Step Toward Latin American Cooperation

Victoria Sordo-Arrioja

> Energy in the physical world is, in a literal sense, the base for change. . . . The essence of economic activity is change, thus, it is energy.[1]

The Latin American Energy Organization (OLADE) in its tenth meeting, held in Panama in December 1979, presented a formal request that the oil-importing countries of the region be guaranteed "a steady supply of oil at official prices."[2] Before the meeting both Venezuela and Mexico had expressed independently their intentions to actively help in solving the energy problems faced by the less developed countries (LDCs), especially those in Latin America, since the oil crisis of 1973.

At OLADE's request, Mexico and Venezuela, the two main oil producers of the region, agreed "to undertake special efforts to meet the demand from Latin American countries who do not have oil in enough quantities."[3] (Both Ecuador and Trinidad and Tobago abstained.) This promise culminated in a formal oil agreement signed by Mexico and Venezuela in August 1980 in San Jose, Costa Rica.

THE AGREEMENT OF SAN JOSE

In the agreement the presidents of the two nations--the Mexican Jose Lopez Portillo and the Venezuelan Luis Herrara Campins--subscribed to a scheme of cooperation open to all oil importers in the region. For those importing nations, two major advantages were stipulated: first, oil supplies to meet domestic demands were guaranteed, and second, preferential credit conditions were granted. After consultation with representatives of the first nine nations to be included in the agreement (Panama, Costa Rica, Nicaragua, Honduras, El Salvador, Guatemala, Jamaica, the Dominican Republic, and Barbados were the original beneficiaries, with Haiti and Belice later included), overall demand in those countries was estimated at 160,000 barrels per day (b/d) to be provided by equal contributions from Mexico and Venezuela.

Favorable credit conditions have been extended to Central American countries so they can work out longer term strategies of energy and development with fewer impingements in the short run. Credit was granted for 30 percent of the market price, to be paid in five years with a low interest rate of 4 percent. However, the term can be extended if the money is used in long-run development projects. Energy projects to explore and develop alternative sources of energy were favored further with an interest rate of only 2 percent and possible extensions of up to twenty years.

An antecedent of this agreement can be traced to September 1979, when Mexican president Lopez Portillo presented a world-scale Energy Plan to the United Nations, stressing the need for international cooperation in the energy field.[4] Along these lines, and with care not to surpass the country's capabilities, Mexico had been preparing a proposal with Ecuador and Venezuela for a joint aid program for Latin American countries with financial problems. Venezuela had been offering financial assistance to her neighbors since the early seventies. Mexico and Venezuela had occasion to share their views during a meeting of the Latin American Economic System (SELA) held in Caracas in January 1980. There Mexico expressed its intention to offer "considerated prices" to the oil importers of the region. Herrera Campins in turn announced that Venezuela would give special treatment to Central America and the Caribbean in selling oil. Mexico offered then to collaborate in a program "as part of the world-scale Energy Plan formulated before the United Nations."[5]

THE BENEFITS

The San Jose agreement is intended to provide stable conditions with regard to oil supply as well as financial benefits to the small countries of Central America and the Caribbean. These provisions may prove pivotal to those countries given that the future economic development of any country has become increasingly dependent upon its energy consumption. Two elements appear requisite to economic development: first, the ability to exploit and/or purchase energy, and second, access to foreign exchange.

Except in the case of Guatemala, which has recently announced oil discoveries, the countries affected by the agreement have had to import their total crude oil requirements and have no alternative but to continue to do so in the near future. For seven (Costa Rica, El Salvador, Guatemala, Honduras, Jamaica, Panama, and Nicaragua), the aggregate oil bill has more than doubled from 1974 to

1980 (Table 8.1), and it is responsible for some 70 percent (as an average) of their current account deficit in 1979 (Table 8.2).[6]

The benefits of the San Jose agreement in the short run (ameliorating such current-account deficits) are apparent, but the major benefits will undoubtedly accrue in the long run, as energy availability facilitates economic development. Economic development means rapid change and increased energy consumption. The Latin American region as a whole will have to double or triple its current energy consumption in order to bridge the existing gap between the Latin American countries and the industrial nations. Yet currently, among the major geographic regions, Latin America has the most acute dependency on oil as a source of energy (80.8 percent).[7] OLADE executive secretary Gustavo Rodriguez Alizarias maintains that the region will not be able to sustain, much less accelerate, an economic development based on oil.[8] Instead, Latin American governments first must increase and diversify their energy supply from nonconventional sources and, second, reduce the present dependency on hydrocarbons by large-scale utilization of renewable sources of energy. This huge geographic region seems to have enough energy resources to do so. Some experts have suggested that although the Latin American countries taken separately have to struggle in the short and medium term to meet their energy needs, their long-run collective possibilities to expand energy consumption are excellent.[9] However, sharp discrepancies exist among the Latin American countries in size, population, and per capita income as well as in natural resource positions. In an August 23, 1980, announcement, the Venezuelan Minister of Energy and Mines reported that Latin America has an oil surplus of 968,000 b/d relative to its consumption. Mexico and Venezuela are the largest producers of crude oil with almost 5 million b/d, followed by Trinidad and Tobago, Ecuador, and Peru with 700,000 b/d--amounts that exceed their domestic consumption. Bolivia and Colombia scarcely exceed their requirements; Argentina is almost self-sufficient. In contrast, Brazil and Chile have decisive oil deficits, and in eleven countries of the region oil is not produced at all.[10]

In terms of per capita income, the Central American countries are, in general, the lowest income earners in Latin America, with an enormous gap between them and the three largest Latin American countries of Brazil, Argentina, and Mexico. Such a discrepancy in per capita income implies a qualitative distinction with regard to energy consumption. For countries with per capita incomes exceeding $400 (1975 dollars), the main source of energy is oil, with hydroelectric power along with residuals from agriculture ranking second.[11] This order is reversed for countries with per capita incomes less than $400 (1975 dollars): they have as their main source of energy resi-

Table 8.1
Oil Imports of Seven Central American and Caribbean Countries
(million current U.S. dollars[a])

	1974	1975	1976	1977	1978	1979	1980
Costa Rica	35.6	60.0	61.5	88.6	101.2	168.4	201.4
El Salvador	52.0	62.1	64.6	72.6	76.4	114.4	151.1
Guatemala	79.6	69.3	58.3	78.6	87.3	84.5[b]	87.1[b]
Honduras	61.8	63.1	53.8	70.3	76.3	112.8	171.0
Jamaica	192.6	183.4	199.9	241.6	174.9	306.0	383.6
Panama	271.0	323.0	235.6	255.1	208.2	301.6	385.5
Nicaragua	50.9	63.4	56.7	78.0	57.8	57.8	141.4
Total	743.5	824.3	730.4	884.8	782.1	1145.5	1521.1

[a]Converted into dollars with the "ae" rate of exchange

[b]Estimated by the author

Source: International Monetary Fund, *International Financial Statistics*, September 1981.

Table 8.2
Current Account Balance of Central American and Caribbean Countries (million current U.S. dollars)

	1974	1975	1976	1977	1978	1979	1980
Costa Rica	-275.6	-227.2	-214.7	-241.1	-379.8	-570.7	-670.2
El Salvador	-152.5	-120.3	-5.8	-8.9	-289.9	78.0	--
Guatemala	-158.5	-143.6	-276.3	-131.3	-386.1	-332.1	-273.3
Barbados	-21.5	-36.8	-56.6	-52.4	-20.0	-41.0	--
Haiti	-47.0	-62.4	-85.5	-101.0	-112.6	-148.7	-158.9
Honduras	-136.6	-130.1	-118.1	-143.1	-174.4	-218.8	-341.2
Jamaica	-117.0	-310.5	-308.6	-88.1	-112.6	-222.9	--
Nicaragua	-272.8	-201.7	-48.6	-192.6	-34.5	88.4	--
Panama	-220.8	-163.8	-172.2	-153.1	-206.9	-319.0	--
Dominican Republic	-275.7	-111.6	-288.7	-312.7	-429.2	-483.2	--
Total	-1678.0	-1508.0	-1574.9	-1424.3	-2146.0	-2170.0	--

Source: International Monetary Fund, *International Financial Statistics*, September 1981.

duals from agriculture, followed by oil. The distinction issues from the smaller share of industry in economic activity in the lowest income nations. In 1979, the energy consumption of the six Central American nations (Costa Rica, El Salvador, Guatemala, Honduras, Nicaragua, and Panama)--all with per capita GDP less than $400 (1975 dollars)--was primarily constituted by firewood and bagasse, which taken together accounted for 47.6 percent of total energy consumption, whereas hydrocarbons represented 45.3 percent and only 7.1 percent was provided by hydroelectric and geothermal power.[12] (See Figures 8.1 and 8.2.)

Thus, energy consumption and economic development are interdependent. External assistance seems vital if the Central American countries are ever to escape from the vicious circle of low energy availability, inhibited economic development, and consequent constrained research and development of alternative sources of energy. The San Jose agreement is just such an attempt to break the vicious circle. Nonetheless, even though comparatively advanced by Latin American standards, Mexico and Venezuela are still less developed nations with many and complex domestic problems of their own. Disregard for or postponement of attention to their own developmental predicaments may entail severe costs for these two nations.

THE COSTS

Venezuela is a founding member of the Organization of the Petroleum Exporting Countries (OPEC), having a 2.2 million b/d output as the second largest producer in the organization (after Saudi Arabia) and at least 18 billion barrels in proven petroleum reserves. With a population of 17 million and a steady position as a major oil exporter since 1928, this country has enjoyed a financial status substantially different from that of most Latin American countries: it has large foreign currency reserves, estimated at $8 billion in 1980.[13] Nonetheless, Venezuela has become a heavy borrower in the international capital markets.

Since 1975 Venezuela has recycled its petrodollars in the region, helping to solve short-run balance-of-payments problems as well as to finance major development projects in neighboring countries. Venezuela has extended a $100 million grant to Jamaica, provided partial financing of a $64 million hydroelectric project in the Dominican Republic, financed a $100 million bridge in Panama, and made loans to governments such as Jose Napoleon Duarte's in El Salvador and Fernando Romeo Lucas Garcia's in Guatemala.[14] The total amount of Venezuelan foreign aid since 1975 has been estimated at $4 billion; this places the country as the single largest donor in the region, followed by the United States with a sum of $2.9

Figure 8.1

Central American Isthmus: Energy Flows, 1979
(percent)

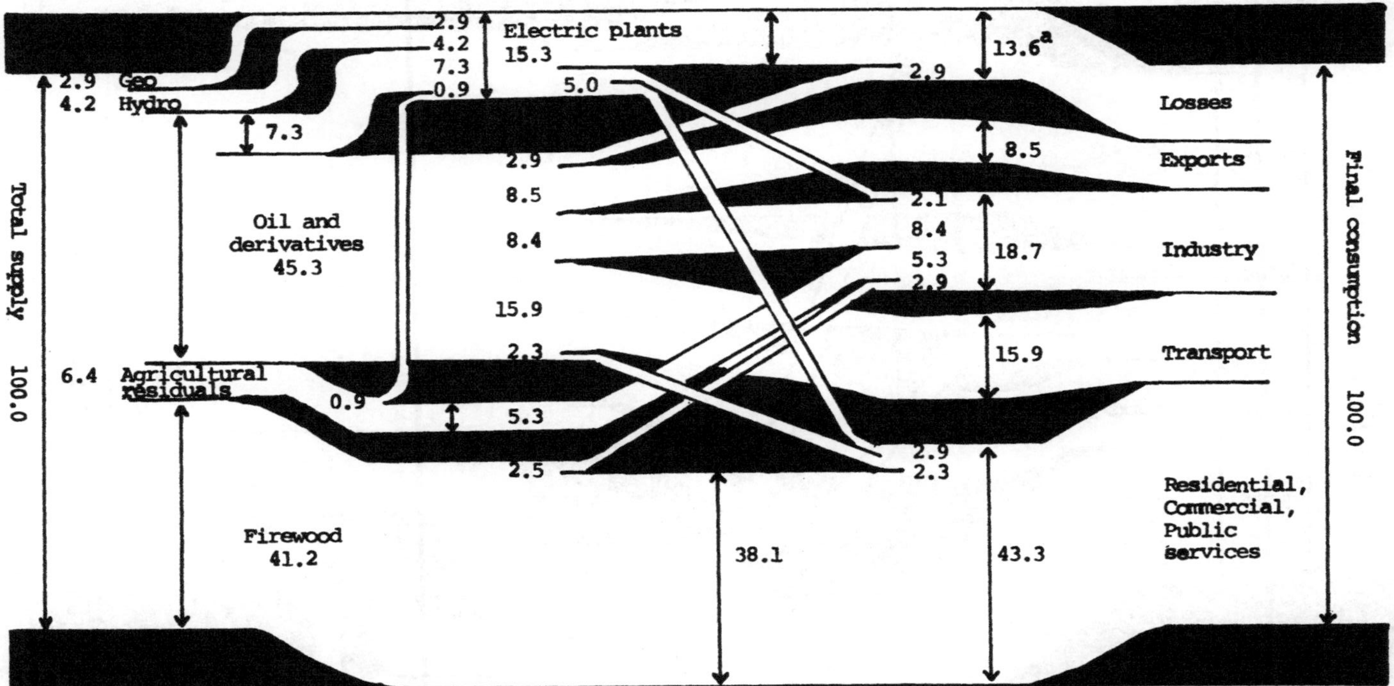

[a] Includes 0.2 percent of losses in coal mines and 0.2 percent of energy left unused from agricultural residuals.

Source: United Nations, Economic Commission for Latin America, Istmo Centroamericano: Estadisticas sobre energia, 1979 (July 17, 1981).

Figure 8.2

Central American Isthmus: Flows of Commercial Energy, 1979
(percent)

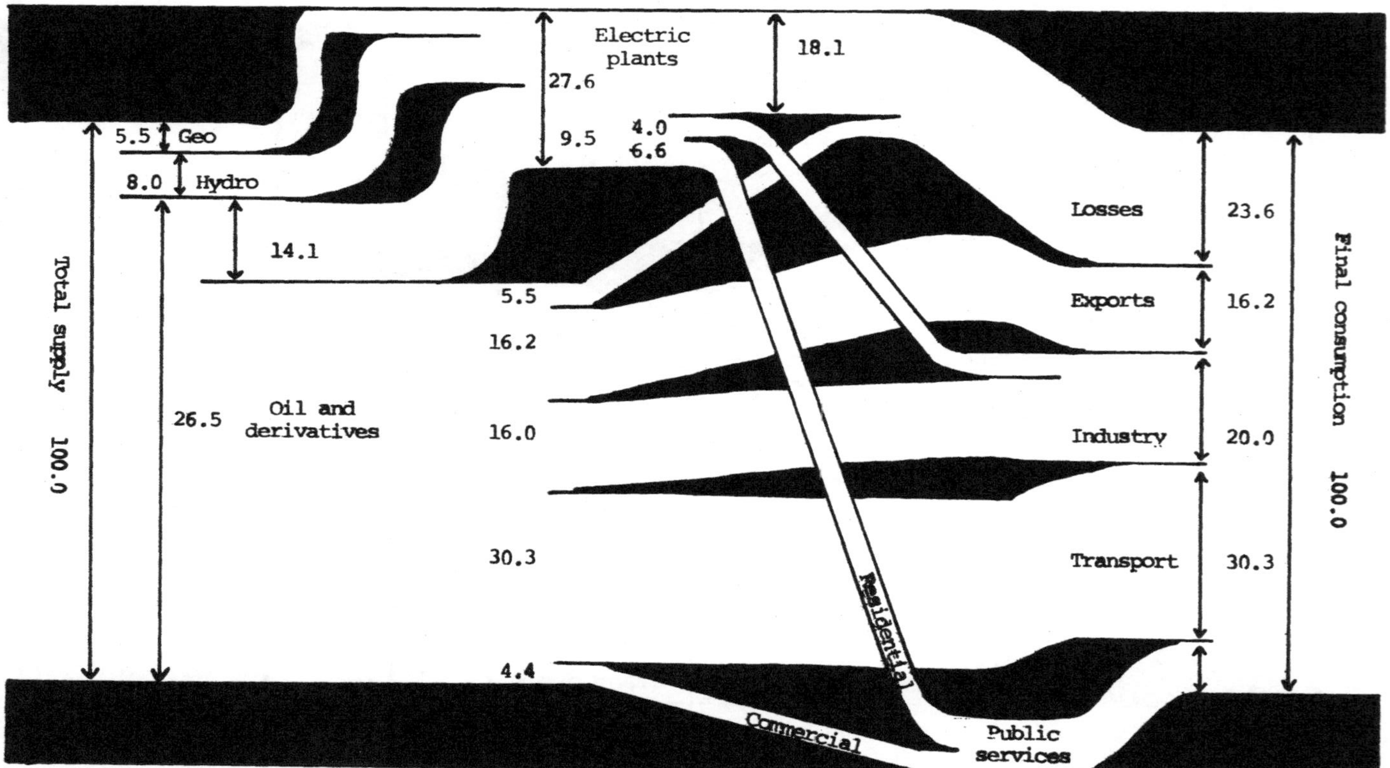

Source: United Nations, Economic Commission for Latin America, <u>Istmo Centroamericano: Estadísticas sobre energía, 1979</u> (July 17, 1981).

billion in the same period.[15]

Such foreign aid schemes were conceived in the context of a general policy to avoid many symptoms of domestic financial super-abundance. When oil prices skyrocketed in 1973, the Venezuelan president pledged to "conduct abundance with a criterion of scarcity."[16] But Venezuelans learned to spend every dollar they earn and more.[17] In spite of its large foreign currency reserves, the external public debt of the country rose to $8.2 billion. Three years passed with zero growth, and unemployment affected 7 percent of the active population.[18] Inflation rates rose at 7 percent in 1978, 12 percent in 1979, 21 percent in 1980, and 15 percent in the first ten months of 1981.[19]

Continuation of foreign aid at the level and of the kind extended thus far may prove insupportable. The use of oil exports revenue for low or no return on investment is especially troublesome given that Venezuelan oil reserves might not be as ample as those of other countries. As the fifth largest producer in the world, Venezuela has only 3 percent of the world reserves and even with lowered levels of production[20] the country will only have oil (given the present technology) to export another twenty years. Therefore it is vital that Venezuela use her oil wisely, to assure her own future: the San Jose agreement may impose constraints on Venezuela's national sovereignty.

On the other hand, in the midst of an international oil drought in the 1970s, Mexico was confronted by sudden oil prosperity. This has caught the eye and the imagination of foreign observers (as well as some nationals) up to the point of inspiring extravagant predictions concerning the oil potential of the country.[21] (The official proven reserves are described in Table 8.3.) It is true that Mexico, with a population of 69.4 million, has made spectacular progress from its previous position as a net oil importer in 1976 to its stature as the main oil producer in Latin America and the sixth-ranking exporter in the world, promising to continue as one of the main oil exporters. But the Mexican government has declared its intention to avoid the mistakes prevalent in other oil exporting countries and has embodied the nation's priorities--economic growth, employment, and the prudent administration of hydrocarbon reserves--in a development plan and an energy program. A production ceiling of 2.7 million b/d has been set. This level of production must first satisfy domestic demand; any remaining surplus may be exported.[22]

Under such an export policy, Mexico cannot long afford to limit its foreign exchange earnings by financing foreign aid programs lest she prove incapable of supporting her imports of capital and intermediate goods, essential to her own rapid economic growth. Mexico is now suffering accelerated inflation of about 20 percent per year; "real

Table 8.3
Total Proven Oil Reserves and Production of Mexico (million barrels)

	1971	1972	1973	1974	1975	1976	1977	1978	1979
Total hyrdocarbons reserves (T.H.R.)	5,428	5,388	5,432	5,773	6,338	11,160	16,002	40,194	45,803
Production	306	326	335	402	464	500	545	672	803
T.H.R./Prod.=Years	18	16	16	14	14	22	25	60	57

Source: Jose Lopez Portillo, *Quinto informe de gobierno,* Informe Complementario, 1981.

increases in the cost of food are running as high as 50 percent annually, and housing costs have doubled for many Mexicans in the past year."[23] And Mexico has witnessed a widening in the external payments gap. In 1980 the country's external payments deficit was substantially higher than expected, having grown from $2.2 billion in 1979 to $4.1 billion in 1980 despite a 62 percent increase in exports;[24] in 1981 the gap was further exacerbated to some $10.8 billion.

The current government's dilemma resides in the juxtaposition of a strategy of growth based on capital-intensive and imports-intensive industrialization in a country where unemployment hovers around 50 percent and underemployment is still higher.[25] This dilemma emerged in the early forties and has now been aggravated by the expansion of the capital- and imports-intensive oil sector. Although a food program has been launched to help decrease cereal imports as well as provide employment in the agricultural sector, there is growing public resentment over the fact that Mexico is getting richer from oil but most Mexicans are not.[26] Thus, although eager to show a charitable attitude toward its poorer neighbors with efforts like the San Jose agreement, the Mexican government is obligated to its own poorer citizens and cannot abandon its traditional domestic paternalism, at least in the short run. This obligation may compromise the best intentions of the San Jose agreement.

However, it is worth noting that the agreement currently represents a modest cost for the country. Of a total 1.25 million b/d of oil exports from January to August 1981, only 6.4 percent or 80,000 b/d went to fill the requirements of the Central American and Caribbean countries.[27] Furthermore, they have been receiving crude oil of a heavy specific gravity, cheaper and not well accepted by industrialized countries due to several major disadvantages involved in its refining. (It is harder to refine, requiring additional steps in processing, and yields a lower volume of the more desirable and expensive refined products per barrel of oil.)

During its first year, the San Jose agreement permitted $700 million to be put into medium- and long-term soft loans to the Central American and Caribbean countries. For Mexico, oil sales amounted to some $2.5 million per day, of which $1.8 million was paid and only $768,000 extended in the form of credit. For Mexico then, the San Jose agreement's current opportunity cost (measured in dollars or barrels of crude oil) is not very high, although political factors may eventually change this.

CONCLUSIONS

The Latin American region's long-run possibilities to expand present energy consumption are excellent. With the aggregate energy resources at Latin America's disposal, were the region a single political entity, it would be self-sufficient. But the resources are unequally distributed among geopolitical bodies; in order to achieve the potential benefits, these inequities must be bridged by political agreement.

In this sense the San Jose agreement represents a first step toward regional economic cooperation that is not permeated by the United States' involvement. It has restored some political flexibility in this strategic region, at a time when the U.S. government insists on interpreting a wide range of political controversies in a narrow framework of East-West confrontation.

Finally, if its costs do not overwhelm the political goodwill of the Mexican and Venezuelan governments, this agreement is likely to advance the interests of the Latin American region, provide a model scheme of cooperation, and foster new understanding among Latin Americans.

NOTES

1. Bernard F. Grossling, "El petroleo de America Latina en la crisis energetica mundial," in *El petroleo en America Latina*, ed. El Cid (Caracas: Cuadernos de Ciencia Nueva/2, 1977), pp. 42-43.

2. OLADE, "Prioridad regional para el abastecimiento de petroleo," *Comercio Exterior* (Mexico), vol. 30, no. 1, January 1980, p. 79.

3. Ibid.

4. The main points of the Energy Plan were to guarantee to every nation full sovereignty over its natural resources, to facilitate financing and requisite technology in order to expand and widen current energy sources, to establish an international system of research and technology transfer in the field of energy, and to create an International Institute of Energy.

5. *El Dia*, January 31, 1980.

6. Included in the average 70 percent current-account deficit are Barbados, Haiti, and the Dominican Republic.

7. Grossling, p. 38.

8. OLADE, p. 79

9. Grossling, p. 39.

10. "Asuntos Generales," in *Comercio Exterior*, vol. 30, no. 9, September 1980, p. 968.

11. Grossling, pp. 37-45.

12. United Nations, Economic Commission for Latin America, *Istmo Centroamericano: Estadisticas sobre energia, 1979* (July 17, 1981), pp. 31-32.

13. "Goodwill from petro-power," *Time*, August 31, 1981.
14. Ibid.
15. Ibid.
16. Jesus-Agustin Velasco, "Mexico en el mercado mundial de petroleo; Oportunidades y peligros para su desarrollo," in *Cuadernos sobre Prospectiva Energetica* (Mexico: El Colegio de Mexico, 1980), pp. 38-39.
17. Ibid.
18. "Venezuela esta sumergida en la estanflacion," *Excelsior*, October 23, 1981.
19. Ibid.
20. Venezuela's oil output has been falling, from the peak of 3.7 million b/d in 1970, to 2.5 million b/d in 1975, 2.3 million b/d in 1979, and reaching 2.2 million b/d in 1980. Velasco, p. 37.
21. "Pemex now claims proven deposits of 72 million barrels and potential reserves are thought to be 250 billion barrels, 73 billion more than Saudi Arabia's." "Mexico Manages a Comeback," *Newsweek*, September 21, 1981.
22. Rene Villarreal, "Oil as an Instrument for Development in an Oil-Exporting Country: Mexico in the Eighties," August 1981 (mimeographed).
23. *Newsweek*, September 21, 1981.
24. Marine Midland Bank, "Mexico," in *Latin American Outlook*, August 1981.
25. *Newsweek*, September 21, 1981.
26. Ibid.
27. Average Mexican oil exports (in barrels per day) for the January-August 1981 period were 600,000 to the United States, 200,000 to Spain, 100,000 to Japan, 60,000 to Brazil, 60,000 to France, 60,000 to Israel, 50,000 to Canada, 80,000 to Central America and the Caribbean, and 40,000 to other importers, a total of 1.250 million barrels per day average exports. Jose Lopez Portillo, *Quinto informe de gobierno*, Informe Complementario, p. 235.

9
Oil and Development Plans of the Late Seventies

Gerardo M. Bueno

The importance of oil in the short-term development of the Mexican economy has been examined at length. Less often explored are the ways in which this resource contributes to the establishment of medium- and long-term economic policies and facilitates economic and social development. A purview of the main guidelines for oil policy before 1978 reveals them to be reasonable, if imprecise. Broadly speaking, oil was considered a key to development: an element that would make a more dynamic economic growth possible. It was thought that oil's main contribution would be to eliminate, or at least reduce, the effects of two factors that had restricted the economy's growth capacity in the past. The first was the balance of payments, in which Mexico had traditionally experienced a current account deficit, and the second, public sector savings and spending constraints. Income obtained from production and exports was to be properly used in accordance with national development priorities. This placed implicit yet clear restrictions on oil exports--that the volume of generated exports not outstrip the country's capacity to absorb foreign currency earnings from the sector. Foreign policy objectives included cooperation in the formulation of a world energy plan consistent with the new international economic order (NIEO).

The aim of this chapter is to give an account of the way in which these objectives and guidelines have changed as well as to examine the treatment of the oil question in particular government plans and programs: the Global Development Plan, the more recent Energy Program, and, to a more limited extent, the National Plan for Industrial Development.[1] Moreover, four aspects of these plans will be analyzed: (1) energy policy objectives; (2) production, import, and export goals and projections; (3) use of energy policy tools; and (4) the relationship between the energy sector and the rest of the economy.

ENERGY POLICY OBJECTIVES

Anyone well acquainted with the country's situation cannot help but be somewhat surprised by the almost blind faith that has been placed in oil's ability to solve the nation's problems. The country appears to overestimate itself as an oil nation and to underestimate itself in other spheres of economic activity.

The origins of this attitude can be traced. Following the oil price increases of 1973, great fear arose about their effects on Mexico's balance of payments and its development prospects. These fears were logical in 1974 since the country's oil reserves, although thought to be considerable, were not confirmed. The confirmation that these oil reserves were as large as expected greatly contributed to the country's recovery from the economic and financial crisis of the last quarter of 1976 and the first nine months of 1977. And the size of Mexico's oil reserves and its export possibilities gave to the performance problems of nonoil exports and the significance of foreign debt figures and the public sector's deficits a completely new perspective.

However, expectations concerning increases in oil production and exports were not articulated in a clearly formulated policy. Whereas the official position is that a coherent, perfectly consistent policy does exist, the allegation pervades, in and out of the government, that to date no such policy has been formulated.[2]

As often happens, the truth lies somewhere in between. Realistically, it could hardly be expected that Mexico should already have formulated a clear oil policy when information was just being received about its oil reserves. But two basic, imminently reasonable principles (initially announced by the president) were used as guidelines: first, that oil earnings be used to bring about development, and second, that the ceiling for oil production and export be basically determined by the country's absorptive capacity. These two principles could be said to form the objectives of both the National Plan for Industrial Development and the Global Development Plan.[3] As is often the case in Mexico, once these policy principles had been announced by the president, they became axiomatic.

Although these arguments proved useful in the initial establishment of policy bases, there was a need for more precise definitions not forthcoming until quite some time afterward. On the one hand, as far as the concept of the key to development is concerned, the total sum of earnings that could be generated from oil and alternative ways of utilizing them needed more precise determination. On the other hand, the concept of absorptive capacity needed to be more exactly defined as a function of the general situation of the country. An economy's absorptive capacity may vary: Capacity exhibited under inflationary conditions with a relatively fixed rate of exchange (like those that have prevailed as a result of policies followed to 1981) varies from that offered by conditions of price stability where exchange rates are adjusted to market characteristics.

Only gradual progress was achieved in establishing more precise energy policy objectives and goals for the use of oil resources. The National Plan for Industrial Development proffered a number of policy principles very similar in nature to previous ones. This shortcoming is attributed both to its timing (being published soon after) and because of the absence of a sufficiently clear general view of development prospects.

This shortcoming was not present in the Global Development Plan, published three years later (in 1980); its aims included defining these prospects and specifying the contribution that the different sectors should make to achieve state objectives. However, the Global Plan is unsatisfactory. It is true that frequent reference is made throughout the text to oil, and it is also true that it includes a specific chapter on energy policy, the tenth of twenty-two main policies. This chapter represents practically no conceptual and operational progress in relation to what had been achieved by the beginning of the administration in 1977 when Mexico learned that it had a lot of oil.

Thus, the energy policy chapter of the Global Plan simply repeats what had already been established as axiom, that Mexico should "use oil to bring about economic and social development by assigning the earnings generated by it to our development priorities."[4] Similarly, the chapter on energy[5] omits any attempt to define more precise objectives. Some goals are stated, it is true, but the projections on which they are based can only be termed tentative. One could even go slightly further and question the Global Plan's view of oil's role in the country's economy. According to this view, in fact, the role oil plays is precisely that of a "national panacea." Oil is seen, for example, as the element that will be decisive in achieving greater efficiency, improving public spending, achieving more favorable terms for obtaining foreign technology and financing, making exports more competitive, diversifying markets by exporting other products, developing the capital goods industry, and other equally ambitious plans. Regarding oil production itself, it gives the impression that thanks to higher production levels it would be possible to "reduce the social costs of oil production" and also implement a far-reaching environmental protection policy. Similarly, it would also appear that the mere existence of Mexican oil would make it much more feasible to both formulate and implement a world energy plan that would become the cornerstone for establishing the NIEO. The most substantial progress in defining energy policy objectives did not come about, then, until the latter part of 1980, with the publication of the document for the Energy Program, produced by the Ministry of National Wealth and Industrial Development.[6] Moreover, a statement was made justifying the formulation of the document, declaring it was necessary "to define a national energy program which, on the one hand, would make it possible to make hydrocarbon resources last longer and, on the other, would facilitate the establishment of the type of structure for energy production and consumption which would allow a gradual, orderly transition to a situation in which hydrocarbons would be in short supply."[7]

As far as the objectives themselves are concerned, the program does adequately distinguish between general and specific goals. The general objective is for the program to support national economic development by increasing energy production in accordance with the needs for balanced economic growth. This general objective also involves ensuring that income generated from oil production will be used for priority action.[8] These are the six specific objectives:

1. To satisfy the country's primary and secondary energy needs.
2. To rationalize energy production and consumption.
3. To diversify primary energy sources, with particular emphasis on renewable resources.
4. To incorporate the energy sector into the rest of the economy.
5. To evaluate more accurately the extent of the country's energy resources.
6. To reinforce scientific and technical infrastructure so that it would be capable of developing Mexico's potential in this field and utilizing new technology.

There can be no doubt that, in comparison with the objectives that made reference to the key to development and absorptive capacity, the objectives of the Energy Program represent a considerable degree of progress. Yet, despite this, their relative vagueness cannot be overlooked. For example, if one takes the first of these objectives, that of satisfying the country's primary and secondary energy needs, it is obvious that such needs are directly influenced by both the type of economic policy adopted at a given time and the way the energy policy tools are used. These needs are not established exogenously and it is therefore necessary for other questions to be taken into account, particularly their relation to the social costs of energy production and consumption.

Similar comments could be made about the second objective, which refers to rationalizing energy production and consumption and is also very closely linked to the previous objective. It is one that is often quoted in the energy programs of the developed countries. In Mexico's case it is also necessary that the extent of energy reserves be taken into account--since these determine the role of production and export levels--and the contribution that each different energy source is expected to make.

Strictly speaking, the fourth, fifth, and sixth objectives are not energy policy objectives, although in the case of Mexico their inclusion is totally justified. It seems particularly fitting that they should include the objective of reinforcing scientific and technical infrastructure, the existence of which is often taken for granted in the developed countries and, what is more serious, simply ignored in many of the developing nations.

In short, it could be said that the Energy Program objectives represented considerable progress. Yet more precise indications of what is meant by "national needs" and the "rationalization" of energy were still needed.

The Energy Program also states that priorities, which are grouped together under three main headings, were established on the basis of the program's objectives. These are energy and industrialization, energy and regional development, and energy and foreign trade.

This classification is correct since it avoids the confusion created in the past over "instruments" and "objectives" in discussions concerning how oil income and the development of certain energies could be used to achieve other economic policy objectives. It is clear that the energy program influences other areas of economic activity, but it is also true that the extent of this impact on other sectors of the economy must be determined.

We should, however, make a number of points about the statements given concerning the relationship between energy and the already-mentioned three headings. The first difficulty that arises is that the program leads one to believe that it will have a considerable effect on the capital goods and other industries. However, a distinction must be made between two phases. The first phase is one that existed in the recent past (1977-1981) when oil production was increasing at a very fast rate, and the second, which will probably continue after 1982, in which oil production will increase much more slowly than in previous years. Consequently, if from now on we bear in mind the goals that will be presently indicated, we could say that the effects of energy on the production of capital goods will be mainly felt in the electronics industry and, to a lesser extent, in the oil industry. The statement made in the Energy Program that "major opportunities are emerging in the stages of production which follow oil extraction, such as refining, petrochemicals, and energy-intensive industries"[9] is also questionable. If we temporarily leave out the refining and basic petrochemical industries, it could be argued that factors exist in the secondary and tertiary petrochemical industries and in those that are energy intensive that are considerably more important than "the creation of incentives by means of the rapid growth in the energy sector which the Program presupposes."[10] In fact, the impact of other factors in recent years has caused a drop in the growth of several of these sectors, despite the rapid expansion of energy production and consumption.

As far as priorities in the relationship between energy and foreign trade are concerned, it is also worrying to see further reference to the aid of "exporting hydrocarbons in accordance with the economy's ability to efficiently absorb foreign currency once domestic demand has been met."[11] This priority, which is obviously an inheritance from the past, obscures other more important priorities that have been established in this field. In fact, the priorities contain a statement that oil exports would be used to achieve important international trade objectives concerning trade diversification, technology transfers, and international cooperation. Apart from being relatively new, these aspects all deserve to be explored in greater detail and this is why it is so disturbing to see that the Energy Program places such emphasis on the concept of absorptive capacity. The latter, apart from being extremely vague, is entirely dependent on the type of economic policy followed and the growth prospects of the world economy.

PRODUCTION, IMPORT, AND EXPORT

Until recently, clear production goals had not been composed beyond 1982, although the National Plan for Industrial Development did include a number of longer-term estimates. Original estimates for 1982 forecast a daily output of 2.25 million barrels of crude oil which, if we assume domestic consumption for the same year to be 1.1 million barrels per day (b/d), would give an exportable surplus of between 1.1 and 1.2 million b/d. This goal was modified at the close of 1979 and was sanctioned by the Global Development Plan.

> The ceiling for oil production and exports which has been established is designed to match the country's structure to its needs, responsibilities and present situation. This ceiling specifies a maximum daily output of 2.5 million barrels of crude oil, with a 10 percent flexibility margin to guarantee supplies and exports. This will allow the country to respond to any risk or eventuality without exceeding the production figure of 2.75 million barrels per day.[12]

If one considers that predictions for 1982 show that

domestic consumption of hydrocarbons will be relatively stable, this modification, which at first sight seems insignificant, is in fact very considerable. On the one hand, it actually means that the export goal is increased at a stroke by almost 50 percent when compared to pre-1982 export figures, and, on the other, this increase is coupled with the 200 percent increase in oil prices that occurred in 1980. In other words, the policy makers were speaking about an almost threefold increase in predicted foreign oil earnings between 1980 and 1982. This is why one should not be surprised that, as stated in a very mild manner in the Global Development Plan, this adjustment in oil output and exports "will allow the country to respond to any risk or eventuality."

Moving on from short- to long-term goals, it is a fact that the only relevant long-term ones are those that appear in the Energy Program. The latter have an additional advantage in that they take into account other energy sources.

These projections are based on the following assumptions: (1) an 8 percent average annual increase in the gross domestic product (GDP) during the 1980s, (2) a reserve of 60,000 million barrels--as an initial estimate--which would be increased to an estimated 100 billion barrels of crude oil if probable reserves are actually proven, (3) a maximum technological limit on oil and gas production of between 8 and 10 million barrels of crude oil equivalent per day, (4) a real annual increase of between 5 and 7 percent in international hydrocarbon prices to the year 2000, (5) a gradual decrease in the relationship between the rate of increase in energy consumption and that of the GDP (a drop in the ratio from the 1975-1979 recorded rate of 1.7 to between 1.3--the most conservative estimate--and 1.0--the most optimistic--by the year 1990, and (6) the establishment of export quotas of approximately 1.5 million b/d of oil and 300 million cubic feet per day (cf/d) of natural gas.[13]

Several aspects of the program should be highlighted since they are not properly treated. These aspects mainly concern exports, assumptions regarding the rationalization of energy consumption, and finally, a reduction in the extent of Mexico's dependence on oil as its main energy source.

Exports

As has been mentioned, the general assumption concerning the performance of exports of oil is that these will be maintained at a fairly constant level of 1.5 million b/d and 300 million cf/d throughout the 1980s and probably over a longer period of time. This target was obtained by joint analysis of two situations described in the Energy Program. In the first case it is stated that

> oil is the principal long-term mainstay of the economy. It is assumed that there will be a high rate of elasticity in imports of manufactured goods in contrast to a demand ratio of the order of 2.5 during the initial stages, which will be gradually reduced at a later time. This hypothesis does not seem to be over-exaggerated if we consider recent events in Mexico and other countries which have indiscriminately followed a policy of lowering all barriers to foreign trade.[14]

In the alternative case

> a strategy for promoting industry and agriculture, an actively protectionist policy would be adopted to allow the substitution of imports of capital goods and other inputs and avoid an increase in foreign purchases of manufactured consumer goods. At the beginning, however, plants and equipment needed to firmly establish a sector for the production of capital goods would have to be imported. Initially this would have the effect of increasing imports but would then reduce them considerably. In comparison with the first situation, this more rapid growth in industrial production would allow the country to gain a greater share of foreign markets thanks to rises in productivity and the introduction of new processes and production lines.[15]

Merely comparing what is said about these two alternatives renders it unnecessary to indicate which may be considered the more suitable of the two. Nevertheless, the assumptions they contain are at best questionable.

One might start by referring to the fact that two of the goals stated in the Energy Program and the Global Development Plan in 1979 and 1980 respectively have not been met. For example, hydrocarbon exports now represent more than 50 percent of total merchandise exports (at present they account for more than 70 percent of the same). What is more important is the fact that the considerable increase in the value of oil exports has not been sufficient to offset the current account deficit, which represents much more than the 1 percent of the GDP both documents regard as a maximum.

There are further inadequacies. The argument--presented in terms of two polar alternatives (one, a policy of lowering all barriers to foreign trade, and the other, an actively protectionist policy)--is, at the least, excessively simplistic. The supposition of the National Plan for Industrial Development that once an actively protectionist policy is implemented, all things are possible (that is, with the substitution of imports of capital and other goods, the creation of industrial infrastructure will as if by magic "allow a greater share of foreign markets" to be achieved "thanks to rises in productivity and the introduction of new processes and production lines") is equally simplistic. Here the following questions come to mind: What are these rises in productivity that are supposed to occur? How is it possible for the introduction of new processes and production lines to automatically make it possible to achieve a share of foreign markets when relatively little evidence has been seen of the ability to do so in the past?

The problem, in fact, is considerably more complex. Before one concludes that export volume may be achieved in the way predicted, details must be provided of assumptions concerning levels of protection, degrees of price variation, changes in exchange rates, and other variables. From this point of view, it could be argued that given the extent of protection afforded Mexican industry, what is worrying is that its primary products and manufactured goods have only a small share of international markets. It is unfortunate that these matters have not been studied in detail when the document itself states that "one of the main conclusions which can be drawn from this analysis is that in the period prior to 1982, the volume of hydrocarbon exports established by this government will make it possible to meet the economy's balance of payments requirements at the rate of growth indicated by the Global Development Plan, whatever the type of economic policy adopted."[16]

Rationalizing Energy Consumption

The Energy Program predicts that the rationalization of primary energy consumption will have important effects and that by 1990, it will provide a daily savings of almost a million barrels of crude oil. There is certainly room for rationalizing energy consumption since the rate that exists in Mexico between increases in energy consumption and the growth of the GDP, which is approximately 1.7, is too high. However, it is doubtful whether 66 percent of savings could be obtained through the use of direct policy instruments and only 34 percent through indirect instruments as stated in the Energy Program. The former are said to include using energy more carefully, utilizing technology to recycle industrial waste, and using energy-saving technology. Obviously the most important indirect measure is that of energy prices.

This document on energy does not clearly explain that such savings are basically a matter of economizing and not of rationalizing technology. Thus, the assumption is that these measures will be taken independently of economic policy which, as many government statements have declared, has so far encouraged energy to be wasted rather than saved. The program seems, therefore, to rely too heavily on the goodwill of energy consumers, despite international experience that has shown that, on the contrary, direct measures in the form of different types of regulation do not normally have a marked impact on energy consumption. The program, then, also contradicts international experience since it considers price mechanisms to be of secondary importance in achieving energy savings.

Reducing the Dependence on Oil as a Part of Energy Supply

The program rightly insists that sources of energy supplies for domestic demand should be diversified. It is correct that this aim should form one of the objectives of energy policy. Yet here again we have a major problem: This diversification not only depends on goals and forecasts being established but, more importantly, on these goals being achieved in an economically rational manner.

Once again we can see, therefore, the presence of a link between the goals and forecasts that appear in the program and the use of economic policy and policy instruments. The document scarcely refers to this link.

Although the concern expressed in different parts of the program about excessive dependence on hydrocarbons to meet domestic energy demand is necessary, it does not warrant modifying these demand patterns even in the long run. In order to justify such expected changes, energy use priorities must be determined and their respective prices evaluated. Unfortunately, the program is not sufficiently clear about either of these points.

With regard to the first point, it would appear that from the point of view of energy supplies, a similar cost is assigned to energy for domestic, commercial, or industrial uses, public and private transport, intensive and nonintensive uses, etc. Concerning the second point, the relative prices of the different types of energy must be determined in the light of the priorities established with regard to demand and supply possibilities, so that they reflect the real economic costs of these types of energy to the country.

This matter is really quite complicated, as can be seen from the two sets of figures (taken from a study of the World Bank and the Energy Program itself) concerning estimated cost trends for electrical power generation in different types of stations, where capital costs and the type of fuel used are given. On the basis of these figures, the program recommends, for example, that the percentage of thermoelectric plants be reduced in favor of nuclear power stations and coal-fired plants.

If, alternatively, we base cost estimates not on international fuel prices but on present domestic prices, we see that thermoelectric plants rather than other types of plants represent the cheapest option ($0.31/kWh as compared to $0.52/kWh in nuclear power stations). Furthermore, we can obtain a broadly similar result if, instead of using present domestic prices, we take the domestic price of hydrocarbons to be 70 percent of their international price, which is what the program recommends. In this latter case, the cost of power generated in thermoelectric plants would be slightly lower than that produced in nuclear power stations ($0.50/kWh as compared to $0.52/kWh). The advantage held by the thermoelectric stations would increase, moreover, as a function of rises in capital opportunity costs.

The problem can now be seen more clearly; decisions about energy use are determined to a large extent by economic considerations. Consequently, energy policy objectives (or those of any other policy) cannot simply be formulated in terms of what it is hoped to achieve, without justifying and defining the decisions that bring about the desired changes in trends. In short, a distinction must be made between viable objectives and those which are no more than a statement of intent.

THE USE OF ENERGY POLICY TOOLS

We have considered it advisable to distinguish between two types of policy instruments, those that are related directly to the energy sector and those that are indirectly connected with it.

Changes in the use and application of energy policy instruments have only been made possible thanks to a more precise definition of policy objectives. What is more nebulous is the relation that necessarily exists between the use of policy instruments and the macroeconomic policy.

In the field of oil itself, direct measures are linked, first, to matters like exploration, construction of installations, creation of infrastructure, and scientific and technological research and, second, to the functioning of the bodies that make up the sector. Of the different plans, the only document to specifically mention this aspect is the Global Development Plan: it states that "Particular attention will be paid to the efficient management of PEMEX in all its technical, administrative, production, and financial aspects."[17]

Practically no other mention is made of this in any other plan, which may be considered an important omission in the document on energy. There are a number of reasons for this: (1) According to a number of figures comparing fixed assets and personnel numbers in relation to production value (even at international prices), PEMEX is far from being an efficient company; (2) PEMEX's production levels have a great effect on the objective of rationalizing energy consumption; and (3) The amount of financing that this company requires strongly influences the country's situation regarding the total foreign debt. For all these reasons it seems strange, to say the least, that the Energy Program does not specifically consider the goals and plans that could be established for PEMEX and the Federal Electricity Commission, to mention only the most important bodies, regarding efficiency levels and a comparison of the benefits to society of investment made in the energy sector and that made in other areas of the economy. Instead of this, mention is made only of expansion programs and plans. To some extent, then, it could be said that we are playing *Hamlet* without the Prince of Denmark.

The most important indirect instrument is prices which, moreover, play a key role in all energy plans. According to initial statements made in the different development plans, price distortions and other factors exist. However, it was not until recently, with publication of the Global Development Plan, that some policy guidelines were first discussed. These include (1) that prices should reflect the social cost of energy, (2) that distortions should be avoided that encourage an increased use of hydrocarbons, and (3) that the price differential between domestic and international prices should not be allowed to become disproportionate.[18]

Slightly more progress was made in defining these guidelines in the Energy Program. It states, however, that in accordance with the National Plan for Industrial Development, "the policy of promoting industry by providing energy at below international market prices should continue."[19] With regard to hydrocarbons themselves, it states that "a system has been proposed which would take long-term considerations into account, and planned adjustments . . . have been designed to avoid creating disproportionate inflationary effects."[20] The objective is for domestic fuel, petrol, and diesel prices to represent 70 percent of international prices and to practically eliminate the price differential for other oil products in the course of the decade.

Despite these arguments, the problem of carrying out the proposed measures still remains, and this is where, of course, more doubts inevitably arise, because just a glance at the statistics reveals that the real domestic price of hydrocarbons has dropped considerably in recent years. This is due, at home, to the fact that prices in general have risen much faster than the price of oil products, which has remained practically unchanged. In comparison with international prices, the drop in the real price of hydrocarbons in Mexico is all the more evident since the international prices for these products have risen steeply.

The former would not, perhaps, be so serious if, as a result of the arguments put forward both in the Global Development Plan and the Energy Program, the decisions were being enacted that are needed to implement their recommendations. This, however, is not the case. We cannot, therefore, avoid concluding, contrary to the arguments put forward in the Global Development Plan, that (1) the price of hydrocarbons reflects increasingly less the social cost of energy and this gap is tending to increase; (2) the distortions that are being created, rather than preventing an increased use of hydrocarbons in relation to other energy sources, are actually encouraging it; and (3) the price differential in relation to international prices is already becoming excessive. It is obvious that recommendations made in the Energy Program are not being carried out either. According to this document, it was hoped that price policy "which is its most important indirect policy instrument . . . would prevent low energy costs and the system of price differentials from encouraging an incorrect use of fuel and the adoption of obsolete technology."[21]

It is difficult to explain the public sector's reluctance to comply with the recommendations proposed in the Global Development Plan and the Energy Program, which are both documents formulated by that sector itself. On the basis of this, a news magazine revealed the contradictions when it referred to a speech given by the president on November 20, 1980. (Comments in brackets are those of the author.)

> Before me are men and women representing the peasants of Mexico [who do not presumably have cars and cannot benefit from oil subsidies] and, before them, I would like to make a declaration to the whole nation: information and misinformation [presumably of the kind that was used in the IV Presidential Report] have been circulated to the effect that the price of gasoline and diesel fuel is to go up. I, the President of the Republic, declare to you, today, on the occasion of this event, that there will be no increase in the price of gasoline and diesel fuel. [The reason the president gave was that] . . . this is a short-term form of fighting inflation which should now be curbed for the good of the nation.[22]

Our concern about reluctance of this kind inevitably increases when, in spite of the continued explosive growth of energy usage (which makes us, according to the Energy Program, both inefficient and wasteful), not only do other state ministers declare that they oppose a rise in energy prices, but the key official of the executive branch, who formulated the Energy Program and is presumably responsible for carrying it out, does the same.

On a slightly more formal level, various reasons may be found to explain the reluctance to adopt the recommendations and proposals put forward. Basically, two reasons stand out: first, the inflationary effect that a rise in oil prices would have, and second, the notion that the existence of very low domestic energy prices serves as a very important stimulus for industrialization and encourages the economy, particularly the manufacturing industries, to be internationally competitive. However, in view of the relatively simplistic way in which they have been presented, without taking other factors into account, both arguments appear to be dubious and, in fact, the recommendations made in the document on energy and in particularly the Global Development Plan have not been implemented at all.

As regards the argument concerning the inflationary effects of a rise in hydrocarbon prices, it can be said, first, that there has been a general tendency to overestimate this effect and that, in any case, at an initial stage it is not necessary to increase all energy prices to the same extent. Taking this a step further, one might question the statements made by several high governmental officials to the effect that "this is not the right moment" to take action to increase prices since "we are at a stage of relatively high inflation."

On the contrary, precisely the wrong moment to take such an action would be when there is price stability or a considerable drop in the rate of inflation, conditions that are definitely not present. The second, more important, point--since such arguments take into account only one point of view--which is concerned with price rises caused by an increase in costs, is, first, the public sector's lack of resources and its increasing deficits, which have an inflationary effect on the aggregate demand side, and, second, the increasing subsidies for energy consumption, which exacerbate the gap between energy prices and its social costs.

This last fact, in turn, has both an income effect on the consumption of oil products and a price effect on the consumption of other types of goods. In short, the arguments used do not make it clear whether the inflationary effects of a rise in energy prices are more to be feared than the inflationary effects of tax deficits and subsidies for the consumption of oil products. This is even more the case when such a decision is analyzed on the basis not of a momentary situation, but, rather, of a longer period of time.

The second argument concerning the effects of low energy prices on the industrial development of the country, and the competitiveness of industrial products abroad, is principally questioned in the very Energy Program itself. As the latter states,

> It is unbeneficial for the country's economy to continue implementing a policy in which domestic energy prices differ excessively from those existing in the international market. There is a risk of encouraging certain types of production which, although profitable on an individual basis, do not generate aggre-

> gate value for the country, or not as much as if the inputs which they utilize were used for different purposes. . . . Other more efficient mechanisms exist to support national industry than that of maintaining energy prices at an excessively low level.[23]

A problem arises once again since, in contradiction with the proposals put forward in the Energy Program, statements have been made that indicate that maintaining low energy prices would fully compensate for the lack of decisions regarding such "more efficient mechanisms" as are suitably emphasized in the program. This is, first, because although we are dealing with an important input, it is also one that does not affect all sectors of production in the same way. In fact, in the industrial sector, as such, there is a correlation between a high degree of energy consumption and a high concentration of capital. In other words, these are not, with a few exceptions, sectors whose development would most benefit the country in terms of industrial development. The second reason for this is that main decisions regarding industrial policy, in fact, have related in the past, and continue to relate, to direct protection measures, which take the form of tariffs, import licenses, and export subsidies, or indirect measures, which consist of varying the exchange rate and applying price controls.

In this regard, it is clear that the decision--which, in addition, is a questionable one--to maintain the cost of an industrial input at a low level, no matter how important this input may be, is hard to justify in terms of the ambitious objectives assigned to it. Experience has shown that there is a risk that decisions regarding action in other more important spheres are neglected because of the costs for the state of making the above-mentioned decision. This matter is all the more important since several recent studies have revealed both the existence of serious distortions in Mexico's trade protection structure and the fact that the peso is considerably overvalued in relation to the dollar. In the first case, the situation is one in which agricultural, mining, and energy activites as well as the basic intermediate goods industry have no protection, or very little, whereas other industries, particularly the consumer goods industry and the durable consumer goods industry, have a very high level of protection. Thus, there is no relative balance in the system. Moreover, this causes many of the highly protected industries to generate an aggregate value that, when measured in relation to international prices, is practically zero, if not negative. Some studies have estimated that the currency is overvalued by approximately 25 to 30 percent, depending on the variables used, and this also has an effect on the way trade protection is structured.

To conclude, the arguments used to justify the decision to continue reducing the real price of energy in Mexico, or rather maintaining its monetary price in conditions of inflation, are invalid from the point of view of both the economy as a whole and the more specific field of energy policy. This decision is critical to energy policy, since it will simply be impossible to achieve a great many of the established objectives.

As a corollary we should ask: What is the point of formulating, approving, and sanctioning plans if, in the final analysis, the decision-making process regarding key issues remains unchanged, as if such plans did not exist or had not been approved? Obviously, it can be argued that plans or programs are not straitjackets, but does the fact that they are not straitjackets mean that they can be ignored? Of course, the basic idea is that the consequences of plans should be evaluated before the plans are approved and not afterward, when they have been invalidated either by action contradicting them or lack of modification.

THE RELATIONSHIP BETWEEN THE ENERGY SECTOR AND THE REST OF THE ECONOMY

The ties between the energy sector, and, therefore, oil, and the rest of the economy can be seen from two different perspectives: in terms of general objectives and priorities, and, more formally, in relation to their contribution to the development goals that the nation has established.

With regard to the first perspective, there can be no doubt that the way both the Global Development Plan and the Energy Program deal with these matters is unsatisfactory. We recognize, however, that the latter document is more precise; this would seem to be due to the progress achieved in indicating energy policy objectives and priorities.

The relevant sections of the Global Development Plan do no more than indicate the following.

> Energy policy becomes the main key to supporting the objectives of development strategy defined by the government, which will allow Mexico to accomplish its historical project. . . . If we consider the philosophical, historical, political, and administrative antecedents and national priorities, the approach established with regard to energy policy forms a very important part of the Global Development Plan. In this context, the overall set of general aims and the development strategy contained in the plan are absolutely fundamental. The action taken concerning energy policy and the results

obtained through the latter must be evaluated in accordance with those aims and strategies.

The Energy Program achieved a certain degree of progress with regard to these general, almost endless, arguments. However, it neither fully solved the problem nor clearly defined the role that the energy sector is expected to play within the economy as a whole. Apart from the topics that have already been dealt with concerning energy policy priorities (in which most progress has been made), these are basically the main points of the program.

1. The Energy Program bases its main guidelines on the National Plan for Industrial Development.
2. From a long-term point of view, it is possible to distinguish two stages in the country's economic development since the financial crisis of 1976. During the initial stage, oil was, first and foremost, a financial instrument that contributed to meeting deficits in the balance of payments and in public sector bills. During the second, oil, as an instrument, has played a special part in structurally transforming the economy.
3. [Energy policy] should support the Mexican economy's transition from its present state of dependence on hydrocarbons to a stage of self-sustained industrialization.[24]

The kind of problems that arise regarding this type of statement are quite obvious. First, there are problems of omission: The sector's role in the economy, its role in relations between the different industries, the ramifications of priority given to investment in this sector rather than others, and its effect on public sector finances and the balance of trade are not treated. Second, there are problems relating to the assumptions that underlie such a statement. We shall briefly discuss the latter since it would be more fitting to examine the former when trying to formally define the relationship between energy and the rest of the economy.

Point 1 contains the first of the problem assumptions. At this stage of development in the country's planning system, one might assume that the Global Development Plan would be given priority over the National Plan for Industrial Development. Yet practically the only mention made of the Global Plan in the Energy Program appears in the foreword, which is signed by the Secretary of Resources and Industrial Development. The latter states that the Global Plan's existence "enables us to act logically, proceeding from general situations to specific ones and not vice-versa as we had previously been obliged to do." This is not a minor problem. As is the case with the Energy Program, the analysis in the National Plan for Industrial Development is limited to examining links with the industrial sector; little mention is made either of links between the energy and other sectors or of the relationship between energy and other key areas of economic policy.

The second point, apparently a salient argument since it is repeated several times throughout the text, may also be regarded as questionable. First, even if it sounds very favorable from a political point of view to say that there was a "financial" crisis in 1976, it can hardly be said that this had any bearing on the formulation, four years later, of a long-term plan. Our second, and most important, objection is that it is not at all clear how the transition would be made between the stage in which oil is basically "a financial instrument" and one in which it would become a "special instrument in the transformation process." Why is it "special" in the second case and only "financial" in the first? What is the substantial difference between the two?

When we consider the more formal aspects of links between the oil sector and economic policy as a whole, once again we see that the different plans shed very little light on the matter. The fact that these links are not specifically examined can only be considered strange, particularly when we consider the decisive role that oil-generated resources are supposed to play in the balance of payments and public finances. It is also strange given that the National Plan for Industrial Development, the Global Development Plan, and the Energy Program all make frequent reference to quantitative methods and models from which a series of very precise answers to specific arguments is supposedly obtained. Thus, expressions such as "the results of the model show that . . ." are frequently used, without the reader being informed either of the model's specifications and assumptions and of the quantitative results obtained or of the different alternatives that may be obtained through variations in these assumptions.

This reluctance to present a relatively detailed set of projections and the marked preference for qualitative considerations (which, however, are sprinkled with what are supposedly very precise data, "as indicated by the model") are probably partially due to the existence of incorrect figures, and perhaps, even more, to a reluctance to reveal the exact nature of some of the assumptions used. An additional reason is that, after a certain time, such projections and, therefore, the validity of the models and, in particular, of the assumptions, may be compared to real data.

In any case, the lack of considerations in the different plans of the links between the oil sector and the rest of the economy represents an important shortcoming. Moreover, as a number of different analyses and studies, which can surely be found in the respective agencies, show, the problems relating to use of economic policy that arise from such links are crucial to the country's prospects for economic development.

By way of criticism, it can be stated that a number of the very few projections that were made public--such as those concerning oil production and export goals, the percentage that oil exports represent to total exports, the size of the current account deficit in relation to the GDP, and the total public finance deficit--have not been achieved, despite what "the models indicate." But here we have omitted the most important need, which is to explicitly determine the effect of the availability of oil resources on economic policy options and the use of key variables. Without this, even though great efforts have been made in this regard, a part of the management function that plans are supposed to have is lost. This, perhaps, explains the reluctance to adopt decisions that are recommended in the very plans themselves.

Several studies carried out by the World Bank, as well as more recent work by Rene P. Villarreal of the treasury, underline the importance of this subject. Aside from a number of minor objections that can be made concerning the Villarreal work, he is certainly correct in indicating that although resources generated from oil ease traditional growth restrictions, they also create new restrictions for the 1980s and the need, therefore, for a new strategy and new macroeconomic policies. In Villarreal's opinion, these restrictions will take the shape of a savings-investment gap and inflation. The former will be caused by the fact that a "dollar earned from oil export is not, nor automatically becomes, a dollar in national savings." The latter will arise when, as a result of this automatic transformation not occurring, inflationary pressures are generated through spending. Villarreal recommends that the public sector make a greater effort to save and implement an anti-inflationary policy, concentrating on supply, which would be backed by measures to promote production and investment as well as a gradual lowering of protectionist tariffs on foreign trade. He also makes a series of recommendations on import substitution and export promotion strategy.

The Villarreal work contains relatively clear examples of the questions that should be examined. Their relevance cannot be denied, whether or not one agrees with the author's results.

CONCLUSION

The analysis of the oil question presented in the different development plans that have been formulated in Mexico in the late 1970s cannot yet be considered satisfactory. An overall evaluation shows that, although relatively important progress has been made in defining energy objectives and, therefore, objectives for the production and utilization of oil resources, the treatment of aspects concerning the establishment of goals and projections, the use of policy instruments, and the definition of the role that resources generated from oil should play with regard to the rest of the economy is still quite incomplete.

Perhaps one explanation of this is that these are the first attempts at planning and programming for the energy sector that have been made known (other attempts made in the past were not widely publicized). It should also be noted that planning ought to be seen primarily as a continuing process and not as a rigid exercise. However, as we have seen, the most worrying aspect is not the plan's omissions. The most serious problem is that even the program's relatively modest recommendations have not been taken into account in the decision-making process. What we have, then, is a plan that we hope will be valid in years to come. As the Global Development Plan states, oil sales "will enable the country to respond to any risk or eventuality."

NOTES

1. The analysis of the Energy Program is based on Secretaria de Patrimonio y Fomento Industrial, *Resumen y Conclusiones--Metas a 1990 y Proyecciones al ano de 2000* (Mexico City: Secretaria de Patrimonio y Fomento Industrial, November 1980).

2. For example, the leader of the majority in the Chamber of Deputies made a number of statements (although these might have been incorrectly reported by the press) voicing opinion to the effect that Mexico did not know what to do with its oil.

3. Secretaria de Programacion y Presupuesto, *Plan Global de Desarrollo, 1980-1982* (Mexico City: Secretaria de Programacion y Presupuesto, April 1980), vols. 1 and 2.

4. Ibid., p. 79.

5. Ibid., pp. 143-150.

6. Summary and conclusions of the Energy Program are quoted from the text published in *Comercio Exterior*, vol. 30, no. 11 (November 1980), pp. 1262-1266.

7. *Resumen y Conclusiones--Metas a 1990 y Proyecciones al ano de 2000*, p. 15.

8. Ibid., p. 17.

9. Ibid., p. 20.

10. Ibid., p. 21.

11. Ibid.

12. *Plan Global de Desarrollo, 1980-1982*, p. 149.

13. *Resumen y Conclusiones--Metas a 1990 y Proyecciones al ano de 2000*, pp. 23-25.

14. Ibid., p. 25.

15. Ibid.

16. Ibid.

17. *Plan Global de Desarrollo, 1980-1982*, p. 150.
18. Ibid., pp. 148-149.
19. *Resumen y Conclusiones--Metas a 1990 y Proyecciones al ano de 2000*, p.30.
20. Ibid., p. 31.
21. Ibid., p. 59.
22. See *Razones*, December 1-14, 1980.
23. *Resumen y Conclusiones--Metas a 1990 y Proyecciones al ano de 2000*, p. 30.
24. Ibid., p. 13.

10
Some Reflections on Mexican Energy Policy in Historical Perspective

Miguel S. Wionczek

By no stretch of the imagination can Mexico be considered a "new" oil country (as, for example, can Norway or Great Britain). Therefore, a brief excursion into the history of Mexican oil and its role in Mexican economic development since the beginning of this century is germane to understanding the formulation of Mexican oil policies in the 1970s and their probable adjustments to the international and domestic conditions of the 1980s.

When many Mexicans insist that their country is not an "oil country" but a "country with oil," it is more than just semantics and political rhetoric. The distinction serves to remind us that although Mexico was at one point an oil country, its highly unsatisfactory experiences during that first oil period made it most inadvisable for Mexico to repeat them. Mexico was a major oil producer between 1900 and 1930. Its oil exports contributed substantially to the Allied victory in World War I. Moreover, profits from Mexican oil, fully controlled in that period by U.S., British, and Dutch private interests, financed to a considerable extent the rapid expansion of the oil industry in the Middle East and South America in the aftermath of World War I. Not only did no countervailing benefits accrue to Mexico during the third of a century of foreign oil companies' operations in the country, but the companies' presence became a source of serious conflicts--endangering the postrevolutionary political independence, territorial integrity, and economic reconstruction of Mexico. At one point in the mid-1920s, in defending oil exploration titles acquired before the Revolution, foreign oil interests in Mexico waged an elaborate conspiracy campaign of provocations, which, if successful, would have led to military conflict between the United States and Mexico. When this scheme was discovered in Mexico City in the late 1920s and the companies found themselves forced to accept national jurisdiction over their oil concessions, they immediately lost interest in Mexican oil and moved en masse to more friendly, competitive locations, mainly Venezuela.

When nationalization was effected in Mexico in the spring of 1938, foreign oil properties were in a state of abandon, their reserves depleted, equipment run down, and Mexican management and technical personnel nonexistent. Even then, oil companies fought tooth and nail against nationalization by organizing worldwide propaganda against "Mexican bandits" and setting up quite successfully a blockade of Mexican oil exports to all major industrial countries. Only the conciliatory attitude of U.S. President F. D. Roosevelt and the outbreak of World War II in Europe saved Mexico from a major political and economic disaster. These dramatic events sank deeply into Mexico's historic memory; they were largely responsible for the country's petroleum policy from 1940 to 1975, prior to the "rediscovery" of Mexican oil wealth and the brief petroleum boom of 1977 to 1981.

The term "rediscovery" is used deliberately. Since the early 1920s, foreign oil companies in Mexico were aware of the country's great oil potential. Ample evidence to that effect is available in the companies' archives and in the diplomatic correspondence of the period. And some fairly detailed references to the locations of the fields discovered in the 1970s by Petroleos Mexicanos (PEMEX) can be found in the Mexican literature of the 1920s, at the height of the conflict about oil rights between the postrevolutionary state and foreign interests.

Although some sources today maintain that these suspected hydrocarbon deposits could not have been exploited for technological reasons at the time of their first discovery in the 1920s, it is much more probable that--as in other parts of the world at other times--the limited exploitation of oil wealth by foreign interests in Mexico reflected their overall strategies and the contemporaneous discovery of more politically attractive "oil pastures" elsewhere. This behavior by foreign oil companies, at a time when Mexico was still the second largest world oil producer and exporter, contributed considerably to Mexico's image as an energy resources-poor country living under the constant threat of early exhaustion of a major component of its industrialization program. And industrialization, it must be remembered, had been presaged as early as the mid-nineteenth century as Mexico's only way out of underdevelopment and backwardness.

The trauma of 1938, the blockade of Mexican oil in foreign markets, the widespread conviction at home that oil was scarce, and the exigencies of industrialization through import substitution defined Mexico's oil policy during the postexpropriation period. From 1938 onward, Mexican hydrocarbons were to be developed _by_ Mexicans _for_ Mexico with priority given, first, to supplying the manufacturing industry, transport, and other kinds of physical infrastructure with oil at subsidized prices;

second, to augmenting autonomous technological capacity and upgrading oil sector skills; and finally, to improving oil workers' welfare conditions, depressed during the thirty-odd years of foreign control of oil fields and refineries. The threefold task was far from easy in a country in which the demand for hydrocarbons grew during the postnationalization decades at an average of 10 percent per year. Reconstruction of the oil industry involved a host of difficult and often conflicting decisions with respect to allocation of scarce financial resources between exploration, crude production, refineries construction, building of distribution networks, and, after 1960, the establishment of the primary petrochemical industry.

The implementation of overall oil policies defined shortly after the nationalization of 1938 proceeded fairly smoothly for some time. The first detailed study of Mexican development experiences and prospects, undertaken in 1952 by a joint World Bank and Mexican government mission, offers an impressive picture of Petroleos Mexicanos' expansion during the 1940s, achieved without outside assistance.[1] The output of both crude and refined oil in 1950 exceeded that of the nationalization year (1938) by close to 80 percent. Not only were the needs of the domestic market, growing by 9.1 percent annually, fully satisfied, but the oil industry was able to export (in net terms) 24 million barrels of crude to finance capital goods imports and amortize a large part of the debt negotiated with oil companies.

The weak point of the oil industry's reconstruction between 1940 and 1950 was determined to be its extremely modest exploration program, due mainly, the report intimated, to the extremely low domestic prices of oil derivatives. But the report concluded, "the petroleum problems facing the Mexican economy were not insoluble nor even particularly difficult. It was just necessary to transfer to the oil sector, public investment made in the sectors of lower priority."[2] Noting the entry of the Mexican Federal Commission of Electricity into large hydroelectric projects, aimed at giving a helping hand to the foreign, privately owned public utilities that demanded growing quantities of coal and oil for electricity generation, the report offered a fairly optimistic prognosis for the Mexican energy sector in the 1960s, in spite of the expected very high growth in total energy demand.

The next important study on the medium-term prospects for Mexico's economic development, drawn up in 1957 by the United Nations Economic Commission for Latin America (ECLA), provided a similarly optimistic appraisal of the Mexican energy sector's prospects until 1965.[3] As far as the oil industry was concerned, ECLA emphasized the highly dynamic growth of demand for oil, natural gas, and refined products in response to greatly expanded motor transport facilities and large investments in roads and thermoelectric plants and in industry in general. ECLA's global demand projections for fuels and lubricants for 1955 through 1965 indicated annual growth rates exceeding 9 percent, only slightly below the rates registered in the immediate postnationalization period. Meeting these projected demands was considered feasible, given Mexico's probable hydrocarbon reserves. Modest exploration activities undertaken by Petroleos Mexicanos between 1938 and 1955 increased proven reserves threefold, from 835 million to 2.8 billion barrels. Circumstantial evidence strongly suggested that probable hydrocarbon reserves were much larger.

The ECLA report of 1957 pursued its speculations on that subject much further than any earlier source. "According to some foreign expert sources," it wrote, "Mexico counts sedimentary zones whose total extension compares with those in Texas, and it is possible that the country may be endowed with oil resources as large as any other Latin American republic, including Venezuela. Moreover, it is quite possible that the extensive continental shelf along the Gulf of Mexico contains very sizeable hydrocarbon resources. It is worth mentioning that only in the Middle East, Venezuela, and Mexico were wells producing 3,000 barrels per day drilled in the past few years."[4] Finally, the ECLA stressed that probable reserves of natural gas were being revised upward: more and more gas was being brought to the surface along with oil (if only to be subsequently flared). Although 1950 estimates described 84 percent of Mexico's hydrocarbon reserves as consisting of crude oil, estimates in 1955 described its composition as 61 percent crude and 39 percent gas.

The ECLA's optimistic appraisals--made almost two decades <u>before</u> the "rediscovery" of oil in the mid-1970s--led to a simple conclusion: contrary to traditional beliefs, the Mexican oil problem was not that of scarce hydrocarbon resources but of technological and financial constraints, aggravated more seriously by the domestic fuels pricing policy. In spite of the fact, however, that the availability of energy was vital to Mexico's industrialization strategy, no long-term exploration program was elaborated by Petroleos Mexicanos. Worse still, oil policy degenerated slowly into a sequence of partial decisions aimed at solving the industry's short-term problems. Thus, instead of being incorporated into the broader context of an economic development strategy, the formulation of oil policy was left to the technical experts of Petroleos Mexicanos whose autonomy made any coordinated energy policy action increasingly difficult. Individual policy decisions, as a rule treated by PEMEX on an ad hoc microbasis, were being implemented, often with considerable delay, only when acute shortages appeared in the exploration, production, processing, and distribution fields. Thus, on the one hand, domestic oil industry savings expanded very slowly, and on the other, competition for public investment funds became steadily more acute. The federal government continued, however, to refuse to adjust fuel prices more than nominally in line with increasing PEMEX operational expenses and investment needs. The rationale was simple: the energy sector was to subsidize the industrialization of the country.

Even when a major oil products price revision took place in 1956, expenditures on exploration activities were again slighted in PEMEX's global investment program in favor of expenditure on oil processing and distribution activities in answer to the dramatic expansion of fuel consumption stimulated by the low energy prices policy. Some knowledgeable people in the oil industry explain the paucity of exploration activities in Mexico in the 1960s by technological factors as well: The country did not acquire early enough the capacity to process internally partial exploration data. The processing of these data abroad was neither prompt nor reliable. Furthermore, world hydrocarbon markets were depressed and imports of crude were cheaply and easily attained. Under such conditions, even the increasing allocation of total federal investment to PEMEX during the 1960s, financed by heavy borrowing abroad (once the Mexican oil sector regained its respectability as an international borrower), did not mitigate the steadily growing gap between domestic demand for oil products and domestic supply of crude. As a result, an acute oil crisis developed by the end of the decade, and by 1970-1971, for the first time in its history, Mexico became a net oil importer.

I

Fortunately, domestic fuel shortages and the rapid growth of crude and oil products imports altered Mexico's oil policy prior to the first international "oil shock" of 1973-1974. If Mexico had not responded rapidly in the early 1970s to its domestic oil crisis by devoting considerable financial and technological resources to the search for "new" oil in its territory, the country's economic growth would have been brought to a standstill by 1975 at the latest, if only for balance-of-payments reasons. In the absence of that policy reorientation, the short, albeit serious, political and financial crisis of 1976 would have achieved the proportions of a general national disaster. But on the eve of that crisis, Mexico had not only regained its energy self-sufficiency, it also had the capacity to start exporting crude at short notice and in growing quantities to redress its extremely weak external position (due in part to the defense of its highly overvalued currency).

What must be remembered is that the "rediscovery" of Mexico's tremendous oil wealth in the mid-1970s occurred, in a way, by accident. The original objective to search for new oil was to eliminate energy scarcities which, by the early 1970s, had put domestic industrial development in great peril. At no point had it occurred to energy policy makers of 1970 through 1975 that Mexico should become again, as it was between 1900 and 1930, an export-oriented "oil country," another Venezuela. Mexico's entry onto the international oil scene after the beginning of the administration of Jose Lopez Portillo in late 1976 was the consequence of the high priority given to oil and other energy investment from 1970 onward by his predecessor Luis Echeverria. Echeverria's presumable objectives were to provide industry with cheap energy, to establish a large petrochemical industry, and to keep the remaining newly discovered oil reserves for future domestic use.

Having lived since the beginning of the century with the perception of Mexico as an energy resources-poor country in which oil, a major component of the industrialization program, was in imminent danger of exhaustion, Mexicans were most surprised with the magnitude of the oil reserves discovered between 1972 and 1976. This rapid passage from scarcity to overabundance gave birth to highly exaggerated ideas of making hydrocarbons a centerpiece of the country's future economic development. The expectations created by the oil "rediscovery," once it was confirmed by external expert sources, were grandiose indeed: oil wealth was to offer to the state the economic and social management capacity previously nonexistent, providing the country with practically unlimited financial capacity. The petroleum industry's expansion plans were to make tractable the long-standing problems of low agricultural productivity, skewed income distribution, and economic dependence. Petroleum exports were to permit accelerated and sustained economic growth (at about 10 percent a year), sharply increased investment in key sectors considered the engine of growth, decreased foreign borrowing, and considerable improvement in social welfare. All these dreams were predicated on a view, shared by most energy experts world over in the late 1970s, to the effect that the world energy economy had undergone a major revolution with the help of the Organization of the Petroleum Exporting Countries (OPEC). The limited extent of oil and gas reserves in the face of the continuously growing demand for fuels both in advanced and underdeveloped countries was to guarantee all producers steady expansion in hydrocarbons exports at constantly rising prices. But even the most enthusiastic advocates of Mexico's exploiting its ability to make oil the pivot of development became rapidly aware of the internal and external limitations of such a strategy. The fact that Mexico was a semi-industrialized country offered both advantages and disadvantages to the unexpected oil boom. Economic and financial advantages would be offset by political disadvantages arising from the country's geopolitical position. The concept of the country floating on a sea of exportable oil, an "oil country," was revised to that of a "country with oil."

The formulation of Mexican oil policy in the second half of the 1970s proved to be a particularly complicated political exercise, and a long time will pass before the full history of this episode will be made available to the public, both in Mexico and elsewhere. What can be said at this early stage is that most political actors on the Mexican scene--and there are many more of them than Mexico's foreign observers think--were involved directly or indirectly in the oil policy decision-making process. Moreover, the process itself was much more agitated than one can gather from official documents and scant local press reports. The temperature of the exercise was high because so many issues, ideological and other, and so many conflicting interest groups were involved. At a very early date it was discovered not only that "oil is a mixed blessing," but also that "big oil is a still more mixed blessing" if discovered at the door of the world's largest importer oil-consuming country whose energy sector happens to be controlled by powerful international private interests.

II

During the two years prior to the fixing of global quotas or ceilings for crude and natural gas exports in the spring of 1980 (valid only until December 1982, the end of the Lopez Portillo administration) and the definition of additional guidelines aimed at assuring hydrocarbon export diversification over the same period, a long and complicated national debate raged unabated about the oil boom's blessings and disadvantages. The debate, which went far beyond the role of oil in Mexico's foreign trade relations, covered the whole field of the interrelations between the oil boom and the future of Mexico's society and economy.

The skeptics were pointing to the economic and social costs of what was perceived as an undeniably excessive dependence on oil in Mexico. The opposite school of thought put emphasis on the benefits accruing to the semi-industrial country endowed with large and steadily expanding oil reserves. The division between the skeptics and the enthusiasts crossed traditional political lines. Both schools had followers in the government, in the public and private sectors, and among intellectual elites. The respective lists of real or perceived social and economic costs and benefits of the hydrocarbon wealth were quite impressive.

The negative aspects of the growing presence of oil in the Mexican economy were summarized by the skeptics in eight major points.

1. The increase in the country's overall economic dependence on the North American market.
2. The increasing concentration in the structure of exports in favor of oil.
3. The substantial contribution of the oil sector to internal inflationary pressures, in spite of continuing low domestic prices of hydrocarbons.
4. The slackened pace of modernization and sagging efficiency in the manufacturing industry, which in an "overheated" economy was selling all its output whether of high or low quality and whether needed or not from the development viewpoint.
5. The serious negative effect of the oil sector on the balance of payments due to three reasons: first, the increasing demand for imports by the oil industry itself (reflecting domestic industrial underdevelopment); second, the increasing demand for luxury consumer goods (reflecting an increasingly skewed distribution of income, partly attributable to excessive dependence on oil); and third, the growing demand for foreign loans (reflecting, among other things, the internal problems of oil industry management).
6. The general relaxation in the public expenditure discipline, reminiscent of similar trends in major less-developed oil producers and exporters.
7. The exacerbation of regional development disparities effected by oil industry expansion.
8. The serious ecological consequences of the new oil activities along the Gulf of Mexico and in southeastern parts of the country.

The opposing list of alleged oil benefits was no less impressive.

1. The contribution of the oil wealth "rediscovery" in the mid-1970s to mitigating the general economic and social crisis of the final two years of the Echeverria administration.
2. The security entailed in possessing a long-term ample domestic supply of hydrocarbons.
3. The increasing contribution of the oil sector to the gross domestic product (GDP).
4. The enhanced ability to insulate the economy against abrupt changes in world energy price levels.
5. The considerable expansion of fiscal revenue from hydrocarbons production and exports.
6. The multiplier effect on the demand for domestically produced capital goods and intermediate products.
7. The positive impact of the oil industry on the development of the backward regions in the southeast.
8. The strengthening of Mexico's trade negotiating capacity vis-a-vis the industrial countries.

The debate between the skeptics and the oil boom enthusiasts was rekindled at the close of 1980 by the appearance of the National Energy Program--an analysis of demand and supply of major primary energy sources in the postwar period, an articulation of targets for production of hydrocarbons to 1990, and projections of uses of all energy sources in Mexico to the year 2000.[5]

The National Energy Program set as its major objectives:

1. Satisfaction of national primary and secondary energy needs.
2. Rationalization of energy production and uses.
3. Integration of the energy sector into the general development of the economy.
4. Erudition of the country's energy resources.
5. Enhancement of the scientific and technological infrastructure to permit the development of the country's energy potential and the application of new energy technologies.

The novelty of the Energy Program resided in the fact that it was a first attempt to integrate into a relatively coherent long-term framework all partial "energy policies" (hydrocarbons, hydroelectric energy, coal, and others) previously pursued independently. The weaknesses of the program were multiple. In the first place, the program was based on a view of the world energy economy prevailing at the time of the "second oil shock" of 1979-1980; second, it was the by-product of two immediately prior planning exercises, the Global Development Plan and the National Industrial Development Plan, respectively, which were conceived and formulated at the time of the oil boom at the end of the 1970s and founded on the premise of a sustained 8 percent growth rate for the Mexican economy; third, defending the hydrocarbon production levels previously fixed for export purposes, the program failed to make a sufficiently detailed analysis of the relations between the oil sector and the rest of the economy; fourth, its assumptions concerning rationalization and savings in energy consumption during the 1980s were particularly optimistic; fifth, the attention given in the program to the means of implementing its proposals was inadequate; and sixth, the document was presented as the work of only the Ministry of Patrimony and Industrial Development and no reference whatsoever was made to the participation of the two large public energy entities, namely, Petroleos Mexicanos and the Federal Commission of Electricity, both of which would implement a considerable number of the energy policy measures suggested by the program.[6]

Throughout the entire administration of President Jose Lopez Portillo (and regardless of discussions as to the dangers and advantages ensuing from an increased dependence of the Mexican economy on oil), activities in this field had been given top priority in national economic policy. The participation of this sector in public investment increased from an annual average of 17.5 percent during the previous six-year term of government (1971 through 1976) to almost 35 percent between 1977 and 1981; its participation in industrial production rose from 5 percent in 1976 to more than 21 percent in 1981; production of crude oil and natural gas liquids rose from 1.085 million barrels per day (b/d) in 1977 to 2.554 million b/d in 1981, production of unprocessed natural gas (including the volume of gas flared) from 2.064 million cubic feet per day (cf/d) in 1977 to 4.060 million cf/d in 1981, crude refining capacity from 308,000 b/d in 1977 to 1.270 million b/d in 1981, and exports of unprocessed oil from 202,000 b/d in 1977 to 1.1 million b/d in 1981. This expansion of all sectors of the industry went hand in hand with a constant increase in proven hydrocarbon reserves (crude, gas liquids, and natural gas), rising from 11.2 million barrels in late 1976 to 72 billion barrels by the end of 1981.

Domestic processed hydrocarbon prices remained unchanged throughout the oil boom in spite of rising inflation and the increasing overvaluation of the Mexican peso. A sharp increase was not introduced until December 1981, just prior to the devaluation of the peso the following February. The two previous increases had been introduced in December 1973 and October 1974, respectively, the second consisting of a federal tax of 50 percent placed on petrol prices to the consumer. Consistent with these measures, investments made by Petroleos Mexicanos had to be financed by the net earnings of the company, the transfer of government funds (amounting to less than tax earnings received by the state from the oil industry), and foreign loans. Because demand and prices in the world market continued to increase, as did the country's income from oil (from $1.1 billion in 1977 to $14.6 billion in 1981), this method of financing the Mexican oil industry did not appear to present any major problems. Net oil earnings were channeled into the rest of the economy and the increasing foreign debt contracted by Petroleos Mexicanos, which by 1981 accounted for approximately 30 percent of the total public sector debt, was to be paid for with supposedly ever-higher foreign earnings in the future.

There were but few observers of the Mexican oil scene, both at home and abroad, who did not share the general expansionist euphoria that accompanied the 1977 through 1981 oil boom. But the early signs of the "oil syndrome" suffered by the OPEC countries during the 1970s had become apparent in the Mexican economy as early as 1978 and 1979. Among the symptoms of this syndrome could be detected (1) an increasing balance-of-payments current account surplus of a temporary nature; (2) chaotic and unbalanced growth of the oil sector with the consequent appearance of serious bottlenecks; and (3) accelerated inflation generated by demand and excessive liquidity in a situation of insufficient supply of goods and services. According to Abel Beltran del Rio's analysis, the measures urgently required to mitigate these symptoms were (1) the diversification of the economy through a major effort on the part of the state to expand and modernize infrastructure, implying imports of foreign goods, knowledge, and technology; (2) the opening of the economy in an attempt to eliminate some of the bottlenecks and consequent inflationary pressure; and (3) the design and implementation of a broad policy of subsidies and transfers (or tax relief) for the purpose of redistributing wealth and protecting the population against the effects of inflation. Although not in a position to forecast the ramifications of the sudden increase in international oil prices that occurred at about the time the study was made (in the winter of 1979-1980), the author who detected and delineated the symptoms of the oil syndrome predicted that "oil will unquestionably produce the same symptoms in Mexico . . . as are commonly . . . observed in other countries which are rich in oil."[7]

A few months later, in November 1980, another observer of the country's economic and energy scene pointed out that:

> In response to the high and sustained growth of the oil sector in recent years, the Mexican economy has begun to suffer certain changes denoting a trend similar to that seen in other oil producing countries:
>
> a) an increasing participation of the oil sector in GDP;
> b) changes in the relative prices and reorientation of the factors of production and of scarce domestic resources towards activities related to oil and those sectors producing goods which cannot be put on the international market (mainly services and construction);
> c) the appearance of bottlenecks in key sectors of the economy, especially transport and industrial capacity;
> d) a rapid expansion of imports related to the absence of dynamism in non-oil exports;
> e) high rates of inflation; and
> f) a tendency towards the over-valuation of the national currency.[8]

Between mid-1980 and mid-1981, the oil syndrome took a stranglehold on Mexico due in part to several factors: excessive public expenditure aimed at sustaining the highest economic growth rates in the world in the context of an increasingly sharp world recession; the total loss of control over public and private investment expenditure; the considerable increase in the bill for imports required to provide an immediate solution for the bottlenecks in infrastructure and in the production apparatus and also to satisfy the demand both for basic foodstuffs and for luxury consumer goods (imports for which increasing foreign currency earnings from oil were not sufficient to pay); and the obstinate defense of the parity of the peso. Seen from the vantage of 1982, during which the country's economic growth rate has dropped almost to zero, these policies confirmed the costs of Mexico's progressively increasing dependence on oil but few of the advantages. The "oil syndrome" might have persisted in Mexico until the end of the current term of presidential office if, in mid-1981, there had not occurred a major basic change in the world energy situation. Although unexpected in countries with little experience in international oil matters (of which Mexico is one), a drop in crude demand in all industrialized Western countries was anticipated by some observers of the energy scene as early as 1980. This reduction in demand was a consequence of the economic crisis and energy-saving measures, the increasing substitution of oil by natural gas and other primary energy sources, and the stagnation of hydrocarbon consumption in underdeveloped areas (with the exception of the Middle East), all accompanied by the constant increase of hydrocarbons supply and other fuels on a world scale.[9]

III

Events over the past twelve months of 1982, taking the country from an 8 percent annual growth rate to zero growth and spawning a series of austerity measures more severe than those introduced in 1976 in agreement with the International Monetary Fund, are too recent to be analyzed in sufficient depth in this chapter. Moreover, this study is restricted to the country's oil problem and its possible future following the breakdown of the "national project" that sought to make oil the hinge pin of long-term economic and social development.

For better or for worse and independent of considerations of Mexico as an "oil country" or as a "country with oil," the extent of its hydrocarbon resources is such that Mexico will continue to play an important part in the international energy scene. However, the country's margin to maneuver abroad with respect to oil under the depressed conditions of the international market is considerably restricted: any serious attempt by Mexico to increase its participation in the foreign market will affect the conditions of the market in the years to come and, in turn, the behavior of the world market will influence Mexican possibilities and limitations in world oil matters. This common-sense rule will continue to be applicable as long as neither of two events occurs: (1) the present world economic crisis ends and a strong and sustained recovery of the industrial economies begins or (2) a new "oil crisis" arises in some part of the world. The possibility that either of these events will occur in the near future is not great.

To those who are of the opinion that Mexico could become a world hydrocarbon supplier on a par with Saudi Arabia because of the magnitude of the former's oil resources, it could be pointed out that, contrary to appearances, even Saudi Arabia is not in a position to follow a completely autonomous oil policy. This is borne out by the fact that Saudi Arabia is losing power within OPEC in spite of its having reduced crude exports from 10 million b/d to some 6 million b/d within a period of less than two years.

The current situation of the world energy market presents Mexican planners with a series of questions of a political and technical nature with respect to both the objectives and the instruments of future oil policy. Among them, the following five are of particular importance.

1. Under the current conditions of the world market, does the fixing of crude export ceilings serve any purpose?

2. If not, what range should Mexico fix (in accordance with the current and potential production capacity of the oil industry) for flexible growth rates of crude exports and processed products and for use as a point of reference in the years to come? These rates should be fixed at levels that neither bring the international market into disequilibrium nor lead to an increase in the already excessive level of foreign debt of the national oil sector.

3. What feasible growth levels should be established for exports of the petrochemical industry, among others, given a recognition that this industry is undergoing a world-scale crisis that is far graver than that suffered by the international crude trade?

4. What type of longer-term oil relations should be established between Mexico and the major importing countries, under the assumption that the diversification of the hydrocarbons trade constitutes an objective of national security for Mexico in order to avoid becoming, by omission, the strategic supplier of crude to the United States?

5. What type of relations would be best to establish with OPEC, since it would not be in the interests of any producer or exporter of Mexico's magnitude to destroy this organization (as is sought by some governments and international oil interests)?

It is obviously not feasible to view the satisfactory solution of these problems only in technical and commercial terms in spite of the short-term weight of these considerations in a country undergoing a serious economic and financial crisis. It is necessarily a political-economic exercise of much broader horizons and one that can be brought to a satisfactory conclusion only if a certain degree of order is introduced into both the foreign and domestic aspects of the national oil industry. (The national oil industry's growth, it will be recalled, has been particularly rapid and uncoordinated, due consideration not being given to productivity, costs, domestic prices, and changes in the structure of domestic demand and thereby contributing considerably to the economic crisis currently suffered by the country as a whole.) This political-economic exercise requires that data and projections of the best possible quality on the conditions and outlook of the world economy be used in combination with analytical capacity of comparable quality.

Not all the costs of the increased dependence of the Mexican economy on oil listed in this chapter have been analyzed in sufficient depth during the course of the final year of the outgoing administration, although there is no doubt that the 1977 through 1981 oil boom has come to an end. The following are some of the subjects, among others, that have been studied in some detail during meetings of the Institute of Political, Economic and Social Studies (IEPES)[10] preliminary to the elaboration of the general policy platform for 1982 through 1988: (1) the increased general economic dependence on the U.S. market; (2) the slackened modernization and reduced efficiency in the manufacturing sector in an economy overheated by the oil boom; (3) the impact of domestic prices policy on the financing of the energy industry, and particularly the oil industry; (4) the impact of oil industry activities on the enormous disparities in levels of regional development; and (5) the ecological consequences of the oil boom along the Mexican Gulf coast and in the southeast.

Nevertheless, with one or two exceptions, other major aspects of the wide range of economic and social costs of the now-past oil boom have been practically ignored as yet: (6) the considerable contribution of the oil sector to the inflationary process; (7) the economic and technical results of accelerated offshore exploration; (8) the failure of attempts to conserve and save energy; and (9) the absence of coordination between Petroleos Mexicanos and the Federal Commission of Electricity.

Each of the nine points listed could be usefully analyzed individually if qualitatively and quantitatively adequate information was available and if the nature of political and technical discourse in Mexico was different. However, as things stand, it is only feasible to put forward working hypotheses as to the roots of each of these problems.

The general increased economic dependence on the U.S. market is due not only to the fact that this is the principal destination of Mexican crude but also to the dominant role played by Mexico's northern neighbor as a source of imports of capital goods (including energy technology), foodstuffs, and luxury consumer goods and the very large number of U.S. transnational manufacturing companies in Mexico. The 1977 through 1981 oil boom served simply to strengthen the invisible economic integration of the two countries begun in the 1940s. This integration was aided by the international economic crisis, the first signs of which originated prior to the Mexican oil boom.

The scant success of attempts to modernize the Mexican manufacturing industry during the 1970s reflects its technological and entrepreneurial backwardness, its aversion to risk in an atmosphere of excessive protectionism, and its access to the public subsidies system, the generosity of which is not to be encountered anywhere else in the world. One of the problems that has not been satisfactorily clarified to date, for example, is why fifteen years after the Mexican state observed the necessity of establishing a capital goods industry, no industry of this nature has made its appearance either in the public or private sector.

The impact of the domestic hydrocarbon prices policy on the financing of the energy industry and on the growth of the country's foreign debt has been examined in detail, although in a very incomplete manner. It would appear that no one is prepared to analyze the problem of the rising costs of the energy sector, clearly because of the fact that this constitutes only part of the economic problem (with respect to the impact of world inflation on the cost of the imports of this sector and the terms of trade with foreign countries), whereas it does have a bearing on extremely delicate domestic political problems, among them--the real cost of projects contracted within the country and the real income of unionized labor.

The role of the oil boom in exacerbating already very unequal levels of regional development and its contribution to the ecological destruction of new oil areas--features that are by no means exclusive to Mexico--have been more closely examined than other issues. Social and ecological damage resulted from the maximum priority given to the programs and projects for new investment formulated in accordance only with the technical criteria of public energy companies, without regard to the social and economic context of the underdeveloped areas where new oil discoveries were made or where new major hydroelectric plants were built.

The question of the oil sector's contribution to the inflationary process, which is only discussed *sotto voce*, must be studied in combination with an examination of the strategy followed by Petroleos Mexicanos between 1971 and 1981--the rate of its exploration, exploitation, processing, and distribution activities and the appearance of bottlenecks within and between these different activities. In view of the fact that the rate of these activities as a whole has most probably been excessive from the point of view of general infrastructure and the availability of equipment in the new oil regions (Tabasco-Chiapas and the Bay of Campeche), the appearance of bottlenecks became inevitable. The same phenomenon occurred at different times in Iran, Saudi Arabia, and Nigeria, to name but a few countries. These bottlenecks were particularly notable in overland transport, storage facilities, ports, and coastal and open sea transport. Further problems arose because of the shortage of exploration and exploitation equipment in both on- and offshore fields, especially when the Campeche continental shelf was opened for intensive exploitation in 1979, its crude production rising twentyfold in scarcely two years (from 52,000 b/d in 1979 to 1.082 million b/d in 1981). A series of emergency programs was implemented to solve these bottlenecks. These programs did not, however, give any consideration to the cost of the physical and technological inputs that would have to be imported. The "race against time" in the new oil areas has proved very costly, although the exact expenditure is as yet unknown. Nonetheless, these costs must influence the investment capacity in other areas of the oil industry.

The full economic and technical ramifications of accelerated offshore exploitation, begun in mid-1979, emerged after a drastic change in the conditions of the world energy market two years later. Crude oil from Campeche is semi-heavy and is therefore for export, whereas the national refining system was designed to process light crude from onshore oil fields. To date, the national market consumes almost exclusively the products derived from light crude even though enormous progress was made during the oil boom in substituting natural gas for oil products, both in Petroleos Mexicanos' processes and for industrial and household uses. Consequently, the interrupted trend of increased domestic energy consumption poses two interrelated problems: a drop in income from semi-processed crude exports (55 percent of total oil exports) and an increasingly limited refining capacity for the domestic market in the context of PEMEX's scarce investment resources.

The most difficult problem is perhaps that of conservation and energy saving within Mexico. In a context in which both electricity and oil are "ours," recent experience has clearly demonstrated that the price elasticity of fuels is close to zero and that incentives to encourage technological innovations for energy conservation do not serve their purpose. The increase of close to 100 percent in petrol (gasoline) and diesel prices to the public, introduced as an emergency measure in December 1981 after almost a year of federal government negotiations, has had no effect whatsoever on the consumption of these fuels and has simply confirmed the inflationary expectations of consumers. The same applies to industrial and household consumption of natural gas, fuel oil, and liquid gas, the prices of which automatically increase 2.5 percent per month (or some 40 percent per annum). Fuel price increases during the last ten years have not only been exceeded by the inflationary process but they fail to take into account the fact that the major users of hydrocarbons are the two large public energy companies themselves whose accounting costs for these inputs are unknown. By way of example, in 1981 Petroleos Mexicanos consumed almost half the natural gas domestically produced and distributed by the same company (excluding gas flared at the wells). About half the electricity generated in the country during the same year was produced from hydrocarbons. In Mexico, energy conservation and saving, particularly after the euphoria of the 1977 through 1981 oil boom, are certainly not merely economic and technological problems. Their roots lie in other aspects of the behavior of Mexican society.

Lastly, the strengthening of coordination between Petroleos Mexicanos and the Federal Commission of Electricity is of utmost importance and urgency in view of the clear historical tendency toward the increased role of oil and natural gas as sources of energy generation in the country. There is no doubt that, with the indefinite postponement of the nuclear electricity plan in 1982, the dependence of the Federal Commission of Electricity on hydrocarbons will continue to increase during the 1980s, notwithstanding the contribution of certain hydroelectricity projects and the increased use of coal for the generation of electricity. The coordination problem between these two giant public energy companies is primarily political in nature. Within the Mexican political system, only the president of the republic can bring about true cooperation between these two bodies whose institutional, bureaucratic, and economic interests do not always coincide as closely as may be supposed.

IV

It is clear from the behavior of the world economy, the downward trends of the international energy market, and the domestic difficulties to which the country is subject that the diversification of energy sources in Mexico is a very remote possibility in the near future. Although increases may be expected in the use of natural gas, coal, and hydroelectric energy during the 1980s, crude oil will continue to constitute the bulk of primary sources of energy. The conversion from oil to alternative nonconventional sources, which made considerable progress in the highly industrialized countries of the West between

1973 and 1981, appears to have slowed down recently because of the abundance of oil and natural gas and the shortage of resources to finance the development of alternative sources of energy. It is not surprising that the same phenomenon has also transpired in Mexico.

Nonetheless, this situation by no means excuses national oil (and energy) policy makers from thoroughly examining three central problems of future policy: first, domestic price levels of oil products; second, the degree of waste in energy consumption apparent during the four years of the oil boom in Mexico; and third, the limits imposed on crude exports by the unstable conditions of world demand.

NOTES

1. Raul Ortiz Mena, Victor L. Urquidi, Albert Waterston, and Jonas H. Haralz, *El desarrollo economico de Mexico y su capacidad para absorber capital del exterior* (Mexico: Nacional Financiera, S.A., 1953).

2. Ibid., pp. 197-198.

3. United Nations, Economic Commission for Latin America, *El desequilibrio externo en el desarrollo economico latinoamericano: El caso de Mexico*, vols. 1 and 2, 1957 (mimeo.).

4. Ibid., vol. 2, pp. 317-318.

5. Secretaria de Patrimonio y Fomento Industrial, *Programa de Energia, Metas a 1990 y Proyecciones al ano de 2000 (Summary and Conclusions)* (Mexico City).

6. For a critical analysis of the Energy Program, see Gerardo M. Bueno, "Oil and Development Plans in Mexico" ("Petroleo y planes de desarrollo en Mexico"), *Comercio Exterior* (Mexico City), vol. 31, no. 8, August 1981, pp. 831-840.

7. Abel Beltran del Rio, "The Mexican Oil Syndrome: First Symptoms, Preventive Measures and Diagnoses" ("El Sindrome de Petroleo Mexicano: Primeros Sintomas, Medidas Preventivas y Prognosticos"), *Comercio Exterior* (Mexico City), vol. 30, no. 11, November 1980.

8. Jaime Corredor, "Oil in Mexico, Summary of Relevant Information and Some Comparison with Other Oil Producing Countries," November 1980 (mimeo.), pp. 26-27.

9. The factors that have led to a radical change in the behavior of the international markets for hydrocarbons and energy in general at the beginning of the 1980s have been analyzed by Miguel S. Wionczek and Marcela Serrato in "Outlook for the International Oil Market During the Eighties" ("Las perspectivas del mercado mundial del petroleo en los ochentas"), *Comercio Exterior* (Mexico City), vol. 31, no. 11, November 1981, pp. 1256-1267.

10. For details, see the pamphlets of the Popular Meeting for Energy and National Development Planning (Reunion Popular para la Planeacion de Energeticos y

Desarrollo Nacional), Institute of Political, Economic and Social Studies (IEPES), Mexico City, May 1982; and Minutes of the Final Meeting of the same cycle, Queretaro, Mexico, May 29, 1982.

Acronyms and Abbreviations

AEC	U.S. Atomic Energy Commission
AGR	advanced gas reactor
API	American Petroleum Institute
A.S.T.M.	American Society Testing of Materials
b/d	barrels per day
Btu	British thermal units
BWR	boiling water reactor
cf/d	cubic feet per day
CFE	Mexican Federal Commission of Electricity
CIDE	Center of Demographic and Economic Research
CICESE	Ensenada Center of Scientific Investigation and Higher Education
cm	cubic meters
cm^2	square centimeters
CNEN	Mexican National Commission of Nuclear Energy
DOE	U.S. Department of Energy
DRI	directly reduced iron
ECLA	United Nations Economic Commission for Latin America; also abbreviated as CEPAL
ft^3	cubic feet
GATT	General Agreement on Tariffs and Trade
GDP	gross domestic product
ha	hectare(s)
IAEA	International Atomic Energy Agency
ICEED	International Research Center for Energy and Economic Development
IIE	Mexican Electrical Power Research Institute

IEPES	Mexican Institute of Political, Economic and Social Studies
IMF	International Monetary Fund
kcal	kilocalories
kg	kilograms
km	kilometers
km^2	square kilometers
KW	kilowatts
kWh	kilowatt-hours
LDC/LDCs	less-developed country/less-developed countries
LNG	liquefied natural gas
LPG	liquid petroleum gas
LWR	light-water reactor
m^2	square meters
MW	megawatts
NEP	National Energy Plan
NIEO	new international economic order
NRC	U.S. Nuclear Regulatory Commission
OLADE	Latin American Energy Organization
OPEC	Organization of the Petroleum Exporting Countries
PEMEX	Petroleos Mexicanos (national oil company of Mexico)
PRM	Presidential Review Memorandum No. 41
psig	pounds per square inch gauge
PWR	pressurized water reactor
SAM	Mexican Food System
SELA	Spanish-Latin American Economic System
SWU	separate work units
SUDUE	Ministry of Urban Development and Ecology
TOE	tons of oil equivalent
UNAM	Universidad Nacional Autonomous de Mexico (National Autonomous University of Mexico)
UNDP	United Nations Development Program
$	U.S. dollars

Index

For Product Safety Concerns and Information please contact our EU representative GPSR@taylorandfrancis.com Taylor & Francis Verlag GmbH, Kaufingerstraße 24, 80331 München, Germany

Batch number: 10726013

Printed by Printforce, the Netherlands